Searching for Schindler

Nonfiction

Outback

The Place Where Souls Are Born

Now and in Time to Be: Ireland and the Irish

Memoirs from a Young Republic

Homebush Boy: A Memoir

*The Great Shame: And the Triumph of the Irish in the
    English-Speaking World*

*American Scoundrel: The Life of the Notorious Civil War General
    Dan Sickles*

Lincoln

A Commonwealth of Thieves: The Improbable Birth of Australia

For Children

Ned Kelly and the City of Bees

Roos in Shoes

Searching for Schindler

a memoir

THOMAS KENEALLY

NAN A. TALESE

Doubleday

NEW YORK   LONDON   TORONTO   SYDNEY   AUCKLAND

Published in the United States by Nan A. Talese, an imprint of
The Doubleday Publishing Group, a division of Random House,
Inc., New York.
www.nanatalese.com

Originally published in a slightly different form in Australia by
Random House Australia, Sydney, in 2007. Copyright © 2007 by
The Serpentine Publishing Co., Pty., Ltd.

Jacket and insert photographs courtesy of Steven Spielberg and
Mrs. Ludmila (Misia) Page

DOUBLEDAY is a registered trademark of Random House, Inc.

Library of Congress Cataloging-in-Publication Data
Keneally, Thomas.
    Searching for Schindler / Thomas Keneally. — 1st ed. in the
U.S.A.
        p. cm.
    1. Keneally, Thomas. 2. Authors, Australian—20th century—
Biography. 3. Authors, Australian—21st century—Biography.
4. Keneally, Thomas. Schindler's list. 5. Schindler's list
(Motion picture) I. Title.
    PR9619.3.K46Z46 2008
823—dc22
[B]
                                        2008015738

ISBN 978-0-385-52617-3

PRINTED IN THE UNITED STATES OF AMERICA

10   9   8   7   6   5   4   3   2   1

First Edition in the United States of America

In memory of Leopold Page, 2001,
and to the continued health of Ludmila (Misia) Page

Author's Note

The author would like to thank Steven Spielberg for permission to use production stills taken on the set of *Schindler's List,* and Mrs. Misia Page for commenting on and correcting the manuscript.

T.K.

Searching for Schindler

One

The Santa Ana winds blow down into the Los Angeles Basin from the north and northeast. They are torrents of air, starved for water in the deserts of Nevada and California. Racing to the sea over the Sierras, picking up heat, dust and spores as they fall, they flow through passes and canyons down into the basin of that great desert city, bringing with them a sense of displacement and filling the air with a strange, malign electricity.

It was late October of 1980, and for me the wind had a curiosity value, a little like an anecdotally useful experience of a slight earth tremor. The heat and bearing of the wind swept me along Wilshire Boulevard as I went out to shop, looking for a modestly priced briefcase in Beverly Hills, unsure that I was in a zone where such banal things were sold. Passing exorbitant Rodeo Drive on my left, one block from the hotel, I saw, stretching away south, a street that seemed to have normal shops, and family cars bearing the scuffs of suburban use. Malls had not yet subsumed the business of such centers as this, and people seemed to be busily parking and seeking out plain, useful human wares.

I had plenty of time to shop. My plane was not leaving for Sydney until the following night. In those days Australia was not a glamor destination, and only a few brave American space travelers joined us natives on the bi- or triweekly planes to the far southwest of the Pacific and my vast native continent, which many Americans still confused with Austria, and whose chief claim to international renown was the lambasting Germaine Greer gave its patriarchy in *The Female Eunuch*.

I had not gone far along the normal-looking street, South Beverly Drive, when opposite a Hamburger Haven I encountered a store named the Handbag Studio. Its goods looked out at me through the glass, out past banners which declared the Handbag Studio's Fall Sale. On these placards, kid skin, cowhide, pigskin, snakeskin and crocodile were mentioned, but above all, discount percentages.

I hesitated, always a nervous shopper. But the shopkeeper soon appeared beside me, having stepped out from within. He had a stocky Slavic look and resembled the great character actor Theodore Bickel—a touch of Tartar in the cheeks, a barrel chest, powerful arms, a wrestler's neck. He wore a white shirt, a conservative tie and a good jacket with an Eagle Scout pin nested in its lapel. There was a glitter of fraternal amusement in his eyes. Even then, I believe I perceived that he had dealt in markets beyond my knowing.

He said, "So it's a hundred and five degrees out here and you don't want to come into my air-conditioned store. Do you think I'll eat you?"

"I was just looking for a briefcase," I said defensively.

"I have the best, young man. Hong Kong and Italy. The best!"

With these assurances, I let myself be led into the store, which—as he had promised—was cool.

"I have a good case," I told him earnestly.

My wife and daughters had given it to me. But one of its hinges had gone, and the other hinge was tearing too. The storekeeper respected my sentimental attachment to the old one, but pointed out that such harm was unlikely to befall what he was offering me. "You just can't put everything in them. A truck? They're not a truck, you know!" And his wide-set Tartar eyes glimmered.

He introduced me to his salesman, a man named Sol. They both had the same sort of Eastern European whimsy, but you could see at once Sol's was of the melancholy rather than the exuberant strain.

As we chatted, the proprietor said, "I must compliment you, sir, on your beautiful British accent."

"Not British," I told him, with an automatic Fenian twitch imbued in me by Irish grandparents. "Australian."

It was true and even fascinating that the Americans, largely ignorant of the bad odor in which our accent was held by the British, unconditionally liked our nearly vowelless English.

"So then," he asked me, "how did a gentleman like you bust your hinge?"

I explained that I'd been at a film festival in Sorrento in Italy.

The Sorrento gig arose from the revival of the Australian

film industry in the early-to-mid 1970s, with directors such as Peter Weir, Bruce Beresford, Gillian Armstrong and Fred Schepisi. Since 1972 I had been associated, as friend and dabbler in film, with Schepisi, then a young Melbourne director, and had even "acted" in Schepisi's first film, *The Devil's Playground*, a far-above-average tale of Catholic childhood and, of course, emergent sexuality colliding with absolutist Catholic doctrine. By that northern autumn, Fred Schepisi had also made a novel of mine, *The Chant of Jimmie Blacksmith*, into a film. The book and film concerned an Aboriginal who in 1900 proceeded on an anti-white rampage in an Australia within whose Constitution, then in its final draft, all reference to the rights of Aboriginals was omitted. I'd played a small part in that film as well, and since Fred Schepisi himself could not go to Sorrento for its biennial film festival, which was devoted that year to Australian cinema, I was invited to go as his stand-in.

They accommodated us in resort hotels along the Mediterranean coast, a festival load of people who had already established themselves and would go on to great renown—Bruce Beresford, the director; Barry Humphries, alias Dame Edna Everage; Judy Davis; Sam Neill; Bryan Brown; Ray Lawrence. We were still, both as a film industry and as a nation, unaccustomed to serious attention in northern European cultural centers, and enjoyed being the plat du jour.

The Italian press treated each film with a heady seriousness, and the showings left time for dining on sumptuous Neapolitan cuisine. But the Italians also gave us a massive

amount of bumf on their industry. This load of serious documents was certainly not the sort of thing one would instantly
throw away, unless one has grown worldly and weary of con-
ferences. Indeed, I think the pages still exist in a storage box
somewhere, a brown archive box unlikely to be opened by me
in this life, and irrelevant to the next. The desire to fit in all the
Italian material had busted the briefcase, one of its two hinges
at the back coming away.

I told all this to the proprietor, who introduced himself as
Leopold Page. I had not long been calling him Mr. Page when
he told me he somewhat regretted the name. It had been
foisted on him at Ellis Island in 1947, where he said they had
scared him by telling him Americans couldn't pronounce his
Polish name, but that if he wanted to change it later, it would
cost him $500. He quickly invited me to call him Leopold; and
then somehow, in a short time, I took to using the diminutive,
Poldek. His true family name from Kraków, that beautiful
Galician city, was Pfefferberg—pepper mountain. I would come
to think it a name that suited his exorbitant energy, his feisty
goodwill.

Having been insistent to get me into his shop, Poldek
seemed more curious about me than interested in a sale. This
was scarcely an act. It would prove to be the way he was. "Do
you know some friends of mine?" Poldek asked me. He mentioned various Eastern European names from Sydney and
Melbourne. No, I hadn't had the honor of meeting these people, I said. "They're Jewish friends of mine," he explained.
"From Kraków and other places." I explained that the Jewish

community in Sydney, though substantial, was not as numerous as in Melbourne.

As we talked, Poldek showed me a simple, lock-up, shining black briefcase, with nicely patterned calfskin. It was spacious and had many compartments. I said I'd take it. I was grateful that the shopping had been uncomplicated and unexpectedly pleasant, and in between chatting, the deal-making had probably taken no more than two or three minutes.

I gave Poldek my credit card, and he put Sol on the phone to call the numbers through to the credit company.

As minutes passed without the card being accepted, Sol kept making doleful faces at us. Poldek told him, "Well, keep trying, Sol!"

"I'm trying, I'm trying. They won't talk."

"Give me the phone!"

"You want the phone when no one's on the line?"

"What do you mean 'no one'?"

"I mean they went away to check the card. I mean there's nobody on the line," said Sol, rejecting all assistance. So Poldek turned to me again and, showing he knew the map of the world, asked me how come I was in California on my way back from Italy to Australia.

I had a book out in the United States, I told him. Viking Press. The publishers had asked me, while I was at least in the Northern Hemisphere, to come over from Italy to the States to do a short book tour. Poldek asked me the name of the book. *Confederates*, I told him, and he said, "*My God!* Sol, is that not the same book I just read a review in *Newsweek*?"

"How should I know what you read?" asked dyspeptic Sol.

I might have doubted Poldek's claim to have seen reviews, except that there *had* been a review in *Newsweek*. With the false modesty of the astonished author, I confirmed that it was so. "And now, sir, what is your name again?"

I told him.

"Sol, Sol," he called to his hapless assistant, parked on the phone. "This guy's a good guy. Cut ten dollars off that!"

Sol grimaced beneath his mustache, and made a *Don't blame me!* sort of gesture with the hand not holding the phone.

Poldek confided to me merrily, "Poor Sol. He's had a rough life."

I was by now such a cherished fellow in the eyes of Mr. Leopold Page that he called his son Freddy to come over from the wholesale warehouse and meet me. Turning up a few minutes later, Freddy proved to be a muscular American boy, impeccably dressed for business. He was highly courteous, however, and softly spoken, and at one stage, as Sol continued his labors with MasterCard, muttered a few items of business to his father.

"Oh, what does he think?" rumbled Poldek to his son, obviously referring to some client. "If he thinks he can get them for that crazy price, tell him to try Borsa Bella himself. To think I started the son-of-bitch off with a special discount! Now he wants my right arm thrown in."

"Okay, Pop," murmured Freddy. "Pop, it's okay. I'll talk to him." It was clear that Freddy had a less pyrotechnic temperament than his father.

Leopold Page turned back to me. "But what am I thinking? You haven't met my beautiful wife, Misia."

The way he uttered the word *beautiful* was full of luscious and emphatic diphthongs. *Bee-ourt-ee-ful*, with the accent on the *ourt*.

At the phone, Sol gave another doleful shrug. "They say they've got to call Australia. There's been all this Australian credit card fraud, they say."

"Give me the phone, give me the phone," insisted Poldek in his jowly basso. "You shouldn't say that sort of thing in front of a gentleman."

Sol handed the receiver to him with a gesture that said, *Go ahead, big shot!*

"Hello," said Poldek Page/Pfefferberg. "What is your name? Barbara. Barbara, darling, you sound like a beautiful woman. I know you have your job. But this man in my store is a gentleman all the way from Australia! Do you want to kill my business, Barbara? I know you don't. But do I need to put up a sign saying, *Australians, Keep Away!*? Yes, I know you're doing your best, but my customer has an appointment to go to. Can you help him along? He's a writer and his schedule's tight. Don't do this to him, Barbara, darling. Make it quick is what I beg. I'll put you back to Sol now, darling. This is Sol."

He handed the phone back to a mournfully gratified Sol. He then moved to me with his hands spread placatingly. "It is a crazy world, Mr. Thomas." He pronounced my name *Tow-mass*.

"So," he said reflectively. "A writer. What a wonderful thing!

I was a teacher before the war. A professor in the *gymnasium*! But a writer! Do you know Mr. Irving Stone? Irving Stone came to this store once. We have a good reputation around Beverly Hills."

As Freddy the son stood by, awaiting any aphorism I chose to utter, Poldek took me aside, toward the curtain which led into the store's back room. At the curtain, he still talked.

"Here's what I wanted to pointed out . . ." he said in a usage he had made his own. "I know a wonderful story. It is not a story for Jews but for everyone. A story of humanity man to man. I tell all the writers I get through here. Sitcom guys. Reporters for the *Los Angeles Times.* I get famous producers or their wives. Did you know Howard Koch? Howard Koch wrote *Casablanca.* A really nice guy. You see, everyone needs a handbag, everyone needs an attaché case. So I tell everyone I know the greatest story of humanity man to man. Some listen—an article there, a news item here. A beautiful young man I know, executive producer of *Simon and Simon* at Paramount . . . he does what he can. But it's a story for you, Thomas. It's a story for you, I swear."

Every writer hears that exhortation. People without any idea of how long a book takes to write pass on the tale of an amusing uncle or aunt, along with the strange addendum: I could write it if I had nothing else to do. The suggestion is sometimes made tentatively, sometimes with the sincere expectation that the writer will answer, *Wow!* That he will drop to his knees and embrace this jewel of a story. That it will take him a few weeks' leisure to produce the finished manuscript. Issues such as

Who will have creative control? Who will get the chief credit on the title page? What will be the royalty share? Are the children of the eccentric aunt likely to sue? What share of subsidiary rights will the author get?—all these issues and more have not occurred to the generous soul who says, "It's a story for you, I swear."

But I had never heard the words come from the lips of a soul so vivid, so picaresquely Eastern European, so endowed with baritone and basso subtleties of voice and inflection, so engorged with life, as Leopold Page/Pfefferberg.

He waited for me to put up resistance, but I did not yet.

He said, "I was saved, and my wife was saved, by a Nazi. I was a Jew imprisoned with Jews. So a Nazi saves me and, more important, saves Misia, my young wife. So although he's a Nazi, to me he's Jesus Christ. Not that he was a saint. He was all-drinking, all-black-marketeering, all-screwing, okay? But he got Misia out of Auschwitz, so to me he is God."

Freddy was listening to this with a minor nod. It was the family story, as central as a book of the Pentateuch.

"Come back into the repair shop, I'll show you."

Poldek led me through the curtained door. Freddy followed. We came into a spacious room with an open office at the rear. The light in the room behind the store area was factory-dim. A slim, well-dressed woman in advanced middle age was working at a repair table running lengthwise along the room, covered with expensive handbags with broken clasps or hinges, and with pliers and receipt books.

"Misia, darling!" Poldek boomed.

The woman looked up with a faint, even timid frown, like a wife used to having her husband's extravagant enthusiasms imposed on her. Poldek introduced me to her. A beautiful guy, he said I was. I was a writer and he'd been telling me about Schindler. This was the first time I heard that name.

"Oh," she smiled. "Oskar. Oskar was a god. But Oskar was *Oskar* as well."

She gave the sort of smile I would get used to from people who had been under Oskar Schindler's control in one or other of his two Second World War camps. The smile of those somewhat baffled by a phenomenon.

"Tell him, Misia!"

"Schindler was a big guy, beautiful suits, the best," she said. "He was very tall and women loved him. Poldek and I were in his camp."

"But your husband tells me you were also in Auschwitz?" I asked.

She admitted it with a dolorous nod. "Oh, dear sir, I was. It was an accident. They sent our train the wrong way. When one of the girls reached up to the window of the cattle truck to break off ice, she saw the sun was in the wrong place for us to be going south to Schindler's camp. We were going west. *Oświęcim*. Auschwitz. It broke our hearts!"

Freddy, the good son, said, "But Oskar got you out, Ma."

Poldek said, "Oskar sent this *bee-ourt-ee-ful Volksdeutsch* secretary off as a bribe to the SS."

"Poldek," Misia chided. "That's just what some people say . . ."

"Darling Misia, Pemper told me!"

"Well, somehow . . . I don't know . . . he got us out."

Just the same, one could tell she had her ideas about it.

"The best journey of my life," she said. "Out of Auschwitz. Half of us with scarlet fever or the typhus. And we turned up at Brinnlitz at dawn, a freezing day, and we see Oskar standing in the courtyard of the factory in a little hat . . . a . . . Poldek, help me."

"In one of those Tyrolean hats, you know, with the feather on the side."

"Yes, a Tyrolean hat. There were SS all about, but we had eyes just for him. He was beautiful. And he told us there was soup."

"Otherwise," said Freddy, "*I* wouldn't be here, would I, Ma?"

"Exactly right, Freddy darlink."

Misia had, like her husband and many Polish-Jewish characters, the tendency to put a *k* on the end of darling. Who was I to talk? My Irish granny, Katie Keneally, had been unable to pronounce a *th* and spoke of *t'roat* (throat) and *cat'edrals*. As for Australians, as a friend would say, our five vowels were *i, i, i, i* and *u*. So Mrs. Misia Page's verbal mannerism had no low-humor effect on me, emerging as it did from the mouth of a woman who had seen the great necro-manufactory of Auschwitz.

Poldek said, "And I wouldn't have had my darling Misia. She is so cute this lady. Too clever for me. She was meant to be a surgeon."

"I'm a surgeon on handbags now," she reasoned. "And I love

it here. Beverly Hills people—some are huffy, you know—but mostly so nice. Excuse me, sir, a second." She moved to Poldek and muttered a few words to him, about problems with a Mrs. Gerschler's handbag and how Poldek might have to replace the whole thing.

"She's got other handbags," Poldek rumbled.

"No, Poldek," Misia said softly. "The poor woman has to take the bag she wants to take. She's been a customer twenty years."

"I suffered every one of them, ai! Si Gerschler . . . such a nice guy married to that shiksa. Tell her, I'm trying to get a replacement one out of the manufacturers. It's on the way."

"Poldek, how can she wear it to the Century City Plaza tonight if it's in a boat somewhere?" asked small-boned Misia, descending into her own guttural range. "I called Mason's wholesale. They have one in stock. They're sending it over to us."

"Misia, darling, that's so expensive and a big write-down."

"We don't have a choice, Poldek."

Misia turned to me and said, "Forgive me. Business, you see." But now it had obviously been settled in the well-practiced way they had.

"Come and see, Thomas, if I may call you," Poldek boomed. "Come and see what I have here."

He led me toward two filing cabinets that stood by the desk at the back of the storeroom, and as he went he settled at top voice with Misia and Freddy the issue of a Bel Air woman's handbag and who would deliver it. Poldek was brought to a pause by the crisis and stopped walking. He sounded bearishly reasonable. "Misia, I have the gentleman here. He's a very famous writer. In *Newsweek* I see his review. If you can call Mason's and get them to deliver it straight to—"

"Poldek, they only deliver retail. You know that. Where's Sol?"

"Sol's on the phone with some MasterCard nebbish. Besides, he's a lousy driver."

"I'll get it there, Pop," said Freddy. "On the way home."

"Could you, Freddy darling? You see, Misia, what a fine boy we made?" And Poldek parted his lips and made a kissing noise, first toward Freddy and then toward his wife.

He opened the two filing cabinets, selecting documents—a piece on Oskar Schindler from the *Los Angeles Examiner*, copies of postwar speeches by former Jewish prisoners made in Oskar Schindler's honor, carbon copies of letters in German, and documents partly yellowed, old enough for the staples in them to have rusted somewhat even in Southern California's desert climate. There was a notice of Schindler's death in 1974, and the reburial of his body a month later in Jerusalem. There were also photographs of scenes from a prison camp. I would discover they had been taken by one Raimund Titsch, a World War I veteran with a limp, the brave Austrian manager of a factory in the terrible camp of Płaszów, southeast of the city of Kraków, from which Schindler drew the laborers for his kindlier small camp within the city.

As Poldek extracted documentation from this drawer and then another, opening and shutting them with gusto, he went on commentating: "This guy Oskar Schindler was a big master-race sort of guy. Tall and smooth and his suits . . . the cloth! He drank cognac like water. And I remember, when I met him the first time, he was wearing a huge black and red *Hakenkreuz*, you know, the Nazi pin."

He riffled through a folder full of photographs and pulled one out, and there was his younger self, very snappy in his four-cornered Polish officer's cap, a stocky boy in a lieutenant's uniform, wearing the same confident, half-smiling face that he now directed at me.

"You see, there! I was Phys Ed Professor Magister at the Kościuszko Gymnasium in Podgórze. The girls loved me. I got wounded on the San River and my Catholic orderly saved my life and carried me to a field hospital. I never forget. I send his family food parcels. Then, after Hitler gave half of Poland to Stalin, we officers had to decide to go east or west. I decided not to go east, even though I was Jewish. If I had, I would have been shot by the Russians with all the other poor guys in Katyń Forest."

Back in Kraków as a prisoner, Poldek had used a German-issued document, which originally had been intended to enable him to visit his soldiers in a military hospital further east, to bamboozle a barely literate German guard. So he slipped out of the railway waiting-room yard and caught a tram and went home to his mother. "And here's this big German guy, handsome, and he's discussing with her that she'll decorate his apartment at Straszewskiego Street. That's how I first met this Oskar Schindler."

By now, Sol had appeared in the doorway of the repair room.

"They came through. The card turns out okay."

"Thanks God," said Poldek. "Now, would you like the brief-case wrapped, sir?"

"No," I said. "I'll carry it with me."

Leopold turned to his patient son. "Stay with the store a while, Freddy. I'm taking Mr. Thomas up to make some photo-static copies."

"Where will you get photocopies this time of day on a Satur-day, Pop?"

"The Glendale Savings. They owe me."

"Wow!" said Freddy, shaking his head.

I said good-bye to Misia Page/Pfefferberg, and we re-emerged into the store. On Poldek's instructions, I left my briefcase there for the time being. I could carry the copies we got made back to the hotel in it. I said good-bye to Sol and Freddy.

We crossed the road and made for the Glendale Savings Bank on the corner of Wilshire. Arriving there at a brisk pace, we queued a time in front of the Enquiries and Transactions counter of the busy Saturday noon bank. At last we reached the counter and a young man attended to us. He called my friend "Mr. Page," confirming that Poldek was indeed well-known at this branch. Poldek handed over his considerable wad of pa-pers. "I need photostatic copies of these, please."

The young man's eyes looked blank. "Mr. Page, you can see it's a very, very busy time."

Leopold did what he would always do when thwarted. He stepped back and raised his hands in a gesture invoking forces greater than this mere transaction.

"So I have lunch with the president every second Tuesday, and you don't have time to give me a few lousy photostatic copies? Is this what you want me to tell your boss? This is an important gentleman." He pointed to me. I had begun the morning as a furtive shopper and was now the center of the gaze of many customers. "He is a famous writer from Australia." Was there such a thing? I looked around in discomfort. "He is here for only one day and a half. So we'll wait." It was clear to the young man that the copies needed, under the pressure of history, to be done *now*.

Cowed by Leopold's portentousness, he said it might take a little time. As I watched the clerk pass on the problem to two women even younger and more flustered than himself, Poldek stepped aside with me to await the copies, and filled me in on more of his history.

Misia had been deported from Lodz in 1939 with her mother, Dr. Maria Lewinson, founder of one of the first institutes of medical cosmetology in Poland. Misia herself had earlier been a medical student in Vienna, and had seen the Führer's triumphal entry into Vienna, and came home to Poland when war began.

"She saw the son-of-bitch, and then he ruined her life. This is how I come to meet a beautiful girl like Misia. And smart. I mean, we were from a good family, my sister and me. But my God, Misia's parents had brains you wouldn't believe. The Nazis deported her mother to Belzec death camp in 1942 and we never saw her again. Why? She had a brain and she was a Jew!

He had longed for Misia, he said, but another Jewish ghetto dweller and former officer had a prior interest, and an officer and a gentleman did not try to court a comrade's girl. But the other man relinquished her and Poldek set out to the Lewinsons' little room in the ghetto to persuade her mother, who considered him a braggart. It took many hours of relentless talk. And then her mother was shipped away and never seen again, and Misia married him.

I asked how he had come to America. After Schindler's factory camp had been liberated by a Russian officer riding a donkey, he and Misia came west into a displaced persons' camp, and he worked for the United Nations Rehabilitation and Repatriation Agency. He had a uniform given him by an American officer, and indeed one could imagine some officer surveying the lines of edgy, fearful former prisoners and seeing something undefeated in Poldek, and putting him into uniform.

Misia and Poldek, having survived and given Schindler the credit for that survival, came to the United States in 1947 and rented a tiny room on Long Island which they shared with other survivors. Poldek saw another Polish refugee repairing handbags in a little temporary store on the pavement. He got talking to the man, and watched him at work, and went home to tell Misia they were now in the handbag business. They did well enough in New York to move out to California in the 1950s, to start importing and to own a few outlets, like the one I had wandered into. That was it. Poldek moved like a man who believed luck was on his side.

The young bank clerk had returned to the counter with the photocopies. He waved to Poldek that they were ready. "I'll pay for these," I offered.

Poldek said, "Are you mad, Thomas? I give this bank all my good business." He accepted the copies from the young man and took his hand for a brief, passionate clasp, as if they had both been into battle together. He waved to the fraught female juniors who were catching their breath further back in the office. "Young ladies! (Aren't they beautiful Beverly Hills girls, Thomas?) Thank you, darlings."

I went back to my cool hotel room with the pile of photocopied papers in my new briefcase. I switched the television to that day's Notre Dame game—I don't remember who they were playing, but I did know vaguely that my grandfather's brother, a great-uncle who settled in Brooklyn, had a son named Patrick Keneally who had gone to Notre Dame on a football scholarship, and this was enough to imbue my viewing with a tinge of partisanship.

With the sound low, I began reading the papers Poldek had given me. It was instantly engrossing material. There was a speech that one of Oskar Schindler's Jewish accountants, Itzhak Stern, made in Tel Aviv in 1963, about his experience working with, as well as for, this Nazi who had been a factory owner. There were a number of other such speeches translated into English from Schindler survivors living all over Europe and the United States. Then there was a series of affidavit-like testimonies from a range of former prisoners, Poldek and Misia among them.

For those who do not know the tale of Schindler, it is briefly stated thus. A young, hulking, genial but not quite respectable ethnic German came to conquered Kraków in 1939 from his native Sudetenland, a part of northern Czechoslovakia where many other ethnic Germans lived. He looked around for business opportunities in Kraków and acquired a factory which he named Deutsche Email Fabrik (DEF), German Enamel Factory. Its nickname among the prisoners who would work there would be Emalia.

As well as sincerely desiring wealth, Schindler was an agent of Abwehr, German military intelligence, an arrangement which saved him from conscription. At DEF he manufactured both for the war effort and for the black market, and developed a symbiotic relationship with his Jews. But to acquire labor, he had to deal with the commandant of the chief labor camp of the area, Płaszów. That is, he bought his labor, at a cheap price, from the SS.

Płaszów concentration camp, on the northern edge of Kraków, was run by the SS man Amon Goeth. Amon was a man very like Oskar, it seemed; of like age, a drinker, a womanizer. In different circumstances, they might have seemed the same sort of man—unsatisfactory husbands, shifty businessmen. The resemblance stopped there, however, for Amon was a killer who pot-shotted Płaszów prisoners with a sniper rifle from his balcony. Where Amon was a figure of terror in the dreams of all the people whose memoirs I read that Saturday afternoon,

Oskar was the improbable savior. His motives were hard to de-
fine, and there were ambiguities to be teased out. But his prisoners didn't care. And neither did I.

Then when the Russian advance of 1944 led to the closure of
Płaszów and DEF, Oskar went to the trouble of founding another camp, near his hometown in Moravia, in northeastern
Czechoslovakia, where his own black-marketeering and the
morally ambiguous deliverance of Jewish prisoners continued.

And so I came across the typewritten list of workers for
Schindler's camp in Moravia, Zwangsarbeitslager Brinnlitz—
that is, Forced Labor Camp Brinnlitz, which was theoretically
under the control of a mother camp, the infamous Gross-
Rosen. Searching through the list, I came upon the names of
Poldek and Misia Pfefferberg. Misia, prisoner 195 on the list,
was recorded as having been born in 1920 and was marked
down as a *Metallarbeiterin*, a metalworker, though she had
never worked with metal until then. Leopold Pfefferberg, another "Ju. Po."—Polish Jew—was number 173 and a *Schweisser*—
welder. He had not used a welding iron until then, but was
confident he could learn. This document, seen by the television glow, representing an acre of safety in the midst of the
huge square mileage of horror that was the Holocaust, would
achieve an international renown as Schindler's list. The list
was life, I would one day write and actor Ben Kingsley would
say, and all around it lay the pit.

I found as well a translation of Schindler's speech, taken
down by two of his secretaries, made on the last day of the war,

addressed to prisoners and to the SS garrison of the camp at Brinnlitz. The sentiments expressed by the tall Herr Direktor of the camp in this speech were extraordinary, with Schindler telling his former laborers that they would now inherit the shattered world, and at the same time pleading with the SS guards who had been ordered to exterminate the camp to depart in honor, and not with blood on their hands. Poldek would tell me that while Schindler gave this finely balanced speech, the hairs were standing up on people's necks. Schindler was playing poker against the SS garrison of his factory-camp, and all the prisoners knew it. But it had worked. The SS drifted away, and left the factory and compound of Brinnlitz, and fled west toward the Americans in Austria.

From these documents concerning Herr Oskar Schindler, I gathered he was a ruined hedonist Catholic. As a former seminarian, and a struggling Catholic myself, I had some time for fellows like Oskar, and little for the over-formal, over-legalistic mediators of Christ who too often asserted that they stood for the real thing. Rudolf Höss, commandant of Auschwitz, had been a good practicing Catholic by legalistic standards and made a lengthy confession before his death. Oskar did not. But Höss was a devourer of souls and bodies, and Oskar, the reportedly lecherous bad husband, was the deliverer. Oskar showed that virtue emerged where it would, and the sort of churchy observance bishops called for was not a guarantee of genuine humanity in a person. Catholic legalism on matters of sexuality evoked sexual neuroses in some men. In others, it produced a dancing-on-the-lip-of-hell exuberance. Schindler was obviously of the latter type, if one can believe the testimonies of all the prisoners who had known him.

Among the testimonies which Poldek had given me, one woman prisoner uttered a sentiment I would later hear from many of his women prisoners. "He was so good-looking and so well-dressed, and he looked you in the eye, and I think if he had asked me for favors, I could not resist. But why should he ask for favors from me, who weighed forty-five kilos, when he was surrounded by beautiful German and Polish girls in the pink of health?"

Some people have always been troubled by Oskar's ambiguity. To me it was from the start the whole point of the tale. Paradox is beloved of novelists. The despised savior, the humane whore, the selfish man suddenly munificent, the wise fool, and the cowardly hero. Most writers spend their lives writing about unexpected malice in the supposedly virtuous, and unexpected virtue in the supposedly sinful. On top of that, the times in which Oskar operated were morally inverted, and so was language. Plain terms—*health action*, *special treatment*, *final solution*, *Aryanization*, *resettlement*, *blood protection*—often meant the opposite of what they implied.

But I doubted I could write a book on this. I was not a Jew. I was a kind of European, but from the rim of the earth. *Après nous les penguins*, I sometimes said in bastard French and as a joke. My father had served in the Middle East in World War II and had sent back Nazi memorabilia—Afrika Korps *Feldwebel* stripes, Very pistols marked with the swastika, a Luger holster similarly stamped—just like the ones the Nazis wore in the Saturday afternoon pictures in the Vogue Cinema in Homebush, Australia.

I remembered, too, the Saturday evening when Aunt Annie minded my little brother, and my mother and I went to the show at the Vogue—at the time, this was the most sophisticated activity possible according to my horizons. It was May 1945, my father was still away and, as far as we knew, about to be shipped to some location in the Pacific's ongoing war. And there on the screen was the newsreel footage of Buchenwald and Bergen-Belsen, liberated by the horrified Allies. There were the corpses, thin and rigid as planks, stacked like so much timber. I could remember the combined shock of the women of that western suburb of war-remote Sydney. The question that hung in the air was: How could anyone have gone to such extremes?

All this was the barest of qualifications to write the book. But then the wonderful aspect of the material, which I saw at once, was that Oskar and his Jews reduced the Holocaust to an understandable, almost personal scale. He had been there, in Kraków and then in Brinnlitz, for every stage of the process— for the confiscation of Jewish property and business, for the creation and liquidation of the ghettos, and the building of labor camps, *Arbeitslager*, to contain labor forces. The *Vernichtungslager*, the destruction camps, had cast their shadow over him and, for a time, subsumed three hundred of his women. It was apparent at once that if one looked at the Holocaust using Oskar as a lens, one got an idea of the whole machinery at work on an intimate scale and, of course, of how that ma-

chinery made its impact on people with names and faces. A
terrible thing to say—but one was not defeated by sheer numbers.

I would find out very soon the reason Leopold Pfefferberg
possessed these documents, and many others as well. As he
had told me, I had not been the only customer to the Handbag
Studio to be fraternally ambushed. In the early 1960s, when
Oskar was still alive, the wife of a well-known and controver-
sial movie producer named Martin Gosch had brought her
handbag into Leopold's store for repair. No doubt with much
loving pouting of lips and praise of Mrs. Gosch's beauty, and
with the handbag as hostage, Poldek had insisted that she set
up an appointment for him with her husband. For a while Mrs.
Gosch found this eminently refusable, but Poldek's powers of
perseverance and undentable charm wore her down. Poldek
told me that when Martin Gosch invited him to MGM Studios
for an interview, the producer had at first chided him for being
so importunate with his wife.

"You must forgive me," said Poldek, "but I am bringing you
the greatest story of humanity man to man."

Martin Gosch had recently tried to make a film about Lucky
Luciano, the mobster, but the Mafia had put pressure on the
project, and the research was ultimately transmuted into a
bestseller, *The Last Testament of Lucky Luciano*, which would be
published in 1974. Gosch had also improbably produced *Ab-
bott and Costello in Hollywood* (1945), and had been a Broadway
producer in the 1940s. Hearing now the Schindler tale from
the lips of a prisoner, Poldek, Gosch was enthused and got to-

gether a team including the screenwriter Leopold had mentioned earlier, Howard Koch, famous for his involvement in the screenplay of *Casablanca* and for having been on the black list of presumed communists during the McCarthy era. In a long life, he would write some twenty-five feature films which would be produced, as well as his ultimately unproduced screenplay of Schindler. His best-known credits included *Sergeant York, Rhapsody in Blue, The Greengage Summer, The War Lover, The Fox*, and the telemovie of Orson Welles's famous broadcast about Martian invasion, *The Night that Panicked America*.

Gosch and Koch began to interview Schindler survivors around the Los Angeles area. Both of them also wanted to meet Oskar, who at the time was living in Frankfurt, largely broke except for contributions from his former prisoners. I would later see in Poldek's storeroom archives a photograph of Gosch, Koch, Poldek and big, bearlike Oskar, sitting around a table, conferring. Oskar's small Frankfurt cement works, funded by the Joint Distribution Committee, a Jewish charity based in New York, had just gone bankrupt in the severe winter of 1962–63, so the idea of film rights must have seemed like rescue. Gosch, Koch and MGM decided that they should ultimately take Poldek and Oskar to meet and gather research from Schindler survivors in Tel Aviv and Jerusalem.

Poldek became de facto archivist for all that was gathered, for every testimony and every document he could corral. For example, the photographs of Płaszów taken by Raimund Titsch, manager of the Madritsch uniform factory inside that horrible camp, were bought by Poldek, in his job of acquiring an archive, in Vienna. The brave Titsch, even eighteen years after the war, was still very nervous of repercussions should it be learned he had kept a secret photo archive. Then Schindler himself supplied documents for Leopold's filing cabinets. More documents were ultimately collected in Israel that year, 1963, when Oskar went back to see many of his former prisoners for the first time since the war.

In Israel, he was given an astounding reception. Itzhak Stern made a speech in which he detailed his intimately perceived version of Oskar's heroism. Hundreds of Oskar survivors gave their testimonies to Yad Vashem, the Memorial and Library of the Holocaust located in Jerusalem, and he was asked to plant his own cedar tree among those dedicated to the small number of rescuers in the Avenue of the Righteous outside Yad Vashem. Among the documents was a picture of Schindler, bulky in a suit, planting his tree. And there were other rewards. A Romanian restaurant near the Tel Aviv waterfront laid on free food and Martell brandy for Oskar.

Poldek had acquired all the associated speeches, official and extemporaneous, given by former prisoners during Oskar's Israeli travels. All the 1963 ceremonies, and the pictures taken by survivors and by Oskar, themselves added to Poldek's ultimate archive, the one I was encountering seventeen years later in his repair shop.

Eventually MGM bought the rights to Oskar's story for $50,000. In the reasonable hope of prolonging Oskar's life, or imposing a saner shape on it, Martin Gosch had written to

Schindler, "I hope the fact that you have taken an apartment in Frankfurt does not mean that you are carrying on with too many women. (One is enough! Remember, dear friend, we are no longer as young as we used to be!)"

Poldek would later claim he made a paternalistic decision to give $20,000 from Oskar's film deal to Mrs. Emilie Schindler, whom Oskar had left and who was living on limited funds in Buenos Aires, and send it to her—I have no reason to believe he was lying—and that he gave the remaining $30,000 to Oskar. Poldek and the Gosches flew to Paris from Los Angeles, Oskar flew from Frankfurt, and they all met in the Hotel George V.

Poldek's version of what happened then was credible only if one had met Poldek and had at least heard tales of Schindler. Here, in 1963, when $30,000 could support even a halfway frugal middle-class family for six years, a sane, single man might have taken the weekend to decide what to do with such a windfall. And, unlike Glendale Savings, the Paris banks closed at midday anyway, and Poldek did not meet up with Oskar till the afternoon. Poldek and his former Herr Direktor/captor, Oskar Schindler, began to track down the names of bank managers. They found one in Clichy. They turned up at the poor man's door as he was preparing for his weekend. They asked him to reopen his bank and cash their check. Of course, his immediate response was no. According to Poldek, they were so persuasive that the man left his suburban home and came into central Paris, and did as they asked. And then Poldek, the former prisoner-cum-welder, and Schindler, the former Herr

Direktor of Zwangsarbeitslager Brinnlitz, went swinging down the Champs, Schindler in an inflammatory, transformed monetary condition.

He paused before a *chocolatier*'s store, where there was an enormous heart-shaped box of chocolates in the window. This was, clearly, not a box for sale—it was the *chocolatier*'s trademark. But Schindler, with characteristic exuberance, could not see the distinction. "I would like to get that for dear Mrs. Gosch," he said.

Even for Poldek, this was too much. "You don't have to, Oskar. This is a box for display. You don't have to get this for anyone. It was enough what you did in 1944."

But Schindler entered the shop and, to the bemusement of its employees, demanded the enormous heart-shaped box in the window. He paid for it, and took it back to Mrs. Gosch in her hotel. Mrs. Gosch did not know what to do with this avalanche of chocolates. But since Oskar was delighted with the gift, so must she appear to be.

The haul of documents Leopold had put together for MGM were what preoccupied and fascinated me that Saturday afternoon in Beverly Hills. For the film had never been made by MGM, and the tale was thus still unknown to the wider world. I had not, as some readers would later kindly see it, fought my way to the center of a maze to emerge with one of the essential tales of an awful century. I had stumbled upon it. I had not grasped it. It had grasped me.

———

About five o'clock, Poldek called to invite me out with Misia and himself, and with Schindler's lawyer Irving Glovin, for dinner that night. I agreed, a little nervously, like someone who was being moved too fast. I told him the material was fascinating but gave him the reasons I couldn't write it. Even as I spoke there was a secret recklessness in me which was open to attempting the thing, for my quite reasonable timidity sat cheek by jowl with my excitement at the challenge and richness of this tale. I had already drawn up a plan of how the book could be achieved. I had just recently been talking to a commissioning senior editor at Simon & Schuster, Nan Talese, who had expressed a desire to publish something by me. I thought that I could approach her, perhaps. It would require a considerable amount to pay for a research journey, for the events of the story had occurred in Poland and the survivors lived in Germany, Austria, the United States, Australia, Argentina and Israel.

Poldek collected me at about 6:30 p.m. in his elegant two-door Cadillac. He was the sort of patriot who always bought American if he could. We were going to dine at a French restaurant in Brentwood.

Unlike Poldek, Glovin proved to have a solemn juridical air, but his wife, Jeannie, a former showbiz singer and dancer, bubbled with a goodwill characteristic of stage people. Glovin had become Schindler's lawyer because he was Poldek's, but unlike Leopold, as the dinner proceeded, with faux French waiters from Central America fussing over Jeannie, who loved it, and Misia, who didn't, Glovin emerged as a determined guardian of the Schindler shrine. There was no doubt he had known and revered Schindler. But while Poldek's Schindler seemed a man in the round, and thus credible, Glovin's seemed a more two-dimensional creature, and Glovin became uneasy with talk about what I loved: Schindler's ambiguity and rascality—the black-marketeering of the produce from his first camp in Poland, his womanizing, the heroic-scale black-marketeering that maintained the operation of the camp at Brinnlitz. He was taken, above all, by Oskar's altruism, and thought it the dominant and only worthwhile aspect of the Schindler story, in the sense that if we could somehow distill what moved Oskar to behave with such goodwill, if we could find the formula for it, we might be able to inoculate the entire human race. Even though he had not been one of Schindler's prisoners, it at once became apparent that he considered himself one of the few legal owners of the story.

Thus it was obvious, as we ate the good food and sipped the good wine, that some financial arrangement would need to be made, some consideration given by me for rights. Because of a strange impetuousness in my temperament, this made me more determined to write the tale, not less. The issue seemed too huge, the story too fascinating, to argue about money. We were discussing the history of the Holocaust, the most fantastical massacre of history, when death was reduced by technology to a manufactured item. I knew that between them, Glovin and Poldek had started a Schindler Foundation, to promote universal tolerance in Oskar's name and to endow a chair and fund research studies into altruism. Whatever its merits, it was a good-faith enterprise. I believed that then and believe it now.

Poldek picked up the bill with cries of, "When we come to Sydney, *then* you can pay!" But for all his assumption that he could claim legal ownership of a story which was in the public arena, Glovin would also prove generous socially.

Already, after less than one day's acquaintance, it was apparent that Leopold had invested much of himself, and his time and cash, promoting Oskar's name and, during Oskar's life, his well-being. Yet with Glovin I was convinced that if I told him what was obvious—that he might not be in a position to claim ownership of all aspects of Oskar's life—he would take legal action to defend his position, and would dissuade Poldek from cooperation. As far as I was concerned, Poldek was entitled to some of the royalties, which I am now even more than then convinced he deserved. After all, he knew where all the contacts were. I was less willing to make a similar arrangement with Glovin, but knew that fighting him legally would be difficult and dispiriting. I was a writer. I did books, not lawsuits.

A wise man might have backed away from the idea of writing the book. I could generally find a viable excuse to avoid writing books I did not want to write anyhow, and that strategy had failed me only once—when Sir William Collins, chairman of the Collins publishing company, persuaded me to write a book to go with a miniseries of which one of the writers was the prolific, restless and brilliant Anthony Burgess. I did the job dutifully, but hated it earnestly. Ironically, it got better reviews than some of my more passionately wrought works.

But if I found a story that besotted me and made me rave to

others about its details, and feel that profound determinism about the need to tell it to other humans, that impulse which is part of the writer's temperament or, some would say, neurosis, then I could be reckless and philosophic about rights and royalties.

Two

In October 1980 when I met Leopold, I had been a writer for some seventeen years or so. I had been a late entrant in life's hectic traffic, having spent six years in a Sydney seminary studying to be a priest. Having left after what I now realize was a crack-up, I was a lost soul teaching high school in Sydney's eastern suburbs, living with my parents in Homebush, and writing during breaks from school. I was studying law too, and would always be something of a lawyer manqué, and as if to compensate for my ineptitude and shyness with women, I coached rugby.

In a room I shared with my brother, a medical student, I had written my first book during the summer school holidays of 1962–63. It was a time when Australians still felt a certain post-colonial sense of cultural unworthiness and yearning. The arts didn't seem to belong much to us. I knew no writers. If there were any, why would they hang around Homebush? Unknown to me, a number of heroic writers, including Dal

Stivens and Morris West, were at the time establishing the
Australian Society of Authors, but that was a poorly reported
event.

We Australians didn't think of ourselves as viable practi-
tioners of writing, for the arts were something which happened elsewhere, in western Europe. Nearly all the literature I
had read came from elsewhere, from landscapes foreign to
me, from seasons which were the reverse of seasons in Australia. The term "Australian literature" would—if uttered in
London by a comedian like Barry Humphries/Dame Edna—
draw fits of hilarity from a British audience, and would be considered amusing even in Australia, like the idea of a dog riding
a bicycle. However, I finished my summer novel in April 1963.
These things can be done while holding down a job if a person
is desperate enough, and I was desperate to find a place in the
world I had once renounced to enter the seminary and was
now anxious to re-find.

I got the name of a publisher's office in London from the
copyright page of a book, bundled up the manuscript as typed
for me by a young woman who lived on the corner of our block
in Loftus Crescent, Homebush, and posted it off. Ten weeks
later I was called out of teaching a class to take a message from
my mother. A telegram had arrived in Homebush from London with the startling news that the publisher wanted to publish me. He (in those days publishers were always *he*), Sir
Cedric Flower of Cassell's, was willing to give me £150 ster-
ling.

In my post-colonial naivety, this was like the finger of the deity emerging from clouds and yelling, "You!" My more urbane British contemporaries would not have seen their own experience of getting published by a trade publisher quite in the same terms—they came from cultivated backgrounds where people did them the favor of telling them that it was impossible to make a living as a writer. But beneath the great dome of the Commonwealth of Australia's then apathy toward writing, I had no one to save me from myself, and I clung to the idea that I would write and survive. This novel was to be my deck chair from the *Titanic*, and I never doubted that, clinging to it, I would be washed to unimaginable places.

So the "profession" of the novel (£150 and all) was my deliverance from a clumsy start in life. That first contract would give me the confidence to reenter the normal, squalling, striving, aspiring world. Among other manifestations of liberation, I would take out and ultimately propose marriage to a splendid and exceptionally beautiful nurse from the Sydney suburb of Leichhardt, who generously considered that my intention to become a full-time novelist made perfect sense. Her name was Judith Martin, and I met her when she was nursing my mother in Lewisham Hospital after surgery. It astonished me that she harbored a preference for me over the doctors and bookmakers who generally took her out. She later said my patter was superior.

We were married in 1965, and in our small house in West Ryde, between Sydney and Parramatta, I began to keep writer's hours, eight to one, two to five, and struggled with the reality that in a suburban house at eight on a weekday morning, writing could seem stupendously difficult, like making a model of Buckingham Palace out of playing cards. I was fortunate that, because of my parents' influence, I was—in the term smart people would ultimately adopt—"task-driven." Now that I was a novelist, I could not face the ignominy of failing to produce novels.

There were a number of factors which enforced discipline on me. One was that the Australian federal government gave me four thousand dollars, then a living wage, as a literary grant for 1966. Coming from a background where men and women viewed industriousness as a prime marker of their existence, I saw that money as coming from taxpayers in hard-pressed homes, and believed a sacred trust had been imposed upon me. It demanded that I consider my new experiment in life as a profession, a daily commitment from me. I must confess I have always tended to have an industrial approach to writing. I knew that if I was to survive I would need to be published as widely as I could manage—a pittance from England, a pittance from America, a pittance from Australia, all adding up to a living.

By 1980, when I met Poldek, I was in mid-career. Some of the early bloom had gone off my repute, at least in the eyes of Australian commentators. By the time I went into Poldek's store, I had two adolescent daughters, Margaret and Jane, and I lived with them and my wife in a house above a beach north of Sydney. I had had the ill grace to forget I had still been fortunate beyond belief—fortunate in the early generosity and openness of readers and, as any writer will tell you, fortunate

in survival. I suffered the self-absorbed and symptomatic dis-
content and restlessness of the writer, which were no doubt
more wearing on my family than on me. But we were happy
and we had come through. And to have a tale before you which
you believed, with whatever degree of self-delusion, that
the world needed to hear, was a splendid, euphoric, ever-
renewing experience.

By the time I walked into Poldek's store I had, through being published in the United Kingdom and the United States,
something of what was called "a cult following," and of course,
ambition still burned and I selfishly yearned for more. Only as
an older writer would I ask, "Who, what god, what destiny,
ever guaranteed that someone who came from Homebush on
the earth's left buttock would grow up to write something people tolerated reading?" I considered the arrival of Schindler's
tale to be part of the sequence of that good fortune. And since I
tried to write more or less a book a year, I was now gripped by
the yearly euphoria that people who did more useful, routine,
albeit more profitable, jobs never had the chance to feel. However, by the light of a gritty, glaring dawn the morning after I
bought my briefcase from Poldek, doubt struck me. How could
I consider myself qualified for this subject matter?

I had read a certain amount about Jewish culture, but I had
only once attended Shabbat in a Jewish house. I knew that
Australia's first Passover had been celebrated with a special
ration of flour and wine in 1788 by Cockney Jewish convicts, as
a result of a Scottish officer in the marines being in love with
one of the young criminals, one Esther Abrahams. That was a

historical curiosity. But Poldek and Misia were the first Holocaust survivors I had knowingly met.

About ten in the morning, Poldek called from downstairs. He had come to take me to brunch. Over the eggs I told him I was a colonial naïf living in a country where one might have expected to find Indonesian settlement if not for its exquisite aridity. It was a place which had been the platform for convicts, minor British officials, gold-seeking British and Irish refugees and postwar displaced persons trying to get as far from pernicious Europe as they could. I knew about Jews chiefly from books—Roth, Malamud, Bellow. Though European by heritage, how could I interpret that full-throated and disordered side of the European soul, full-throated anti-Semitism?

After every objection, Poldek said, "That's good, Thomas, that's good. It means you don't have an ax to grind." And then he'd repeat (constantly), "This is not a book for Jews, this is a book for Gentiles. This is a great story of humanity man to man. An Australian is perfect to write it. What should you know? You know about humans. I'll travel with you, Thomas!"

But the research task suddenly seemed more forbidding than it had the day before.

By Sunday lunchtime, Glovin, Poldek and I were discussing this golden and redemptive tale and the more banal question of who had legal rights, and in what sense, to the Schindler material. Things were getting complex, but were not yet set in concrete. It was agreed that I should go home that night with whatever photocopied documents Leopold had given me, and the addresses of various Australian Schindler survivors and others who knew Schindler. It excited me to think that, through the tragedies of history, there were such people in my own remote country.

I would make contact with the Australian survivors, add what they told me into the mix, and produce—this was my own suggestion—two documents: a fifteen- to twenty-page treatment of the material for my friend the Simon & Schuster editor Nan Talese, and a shorter, two-page abstract in case others didn't have the patience for a full document. After all, Paramount Studios had acquired Simon & Schuster, and I was aware there were executives involved who, ironically, preferred a short précis to a full manuscript. An independent director named Robert Solo, who wanted to make a film of my book *Confederates*, had taken me out to see a Paramount executive just a month or so before I met Poldek. The executive had picked the book up from his desk, weighed it in his hand and said, "Kinda thick, isn't it?" Then he'd commissioned a team of two screenwriters to turn out a screenplay for him—just, it seemed, to deal with his own reading incapacities. The screenplay was written—a good one—but joined the great majority of scripts that are never made into films.

Poldek, of course, insisted on taking me to the airport that night, and also insisted we go to a kosher restaurant on the way, where, engorged already with overrich Californian food, I choked back some latkes on the grounds, stated by Poldek, that "airline food is poison!" I did not yet realize that if you did not agree to something Leopold said, the only way out was to exclaim as fast and hard and loudly as him. I should have said, "You want I should have indigestion all the way to Australia?" Modest resistance, however, and what Anglo-Celts thought of as politeness, never had a chance against him.

"I doubt Irving Glovin is comfortable with me," I said over the kosher food. "He already finds my approach too irreverent."

"Irreverent? What does he know from irreverent? Listen, I saw Schindler screwing SS girls in the water reservoirs at Brinnlitz's factory. That's irreverent."

The flight to Australia leaves Los Angeles late in the evening, and a small technical problem will, and often has, nudge the departure back to after midnight. But that night we took off more or less on time. Poldek's last words to me at the gate were: "Thomas, who will do it if not you? You think I have them queued up?"

The plane taxied past the sign on the runway that says NO TURN BEFORE THE OCEAN—a sign which always rather disturbed me, since I thought that any pilot worth his salt might already know that. Then we travelers were shot straight out over the Pacific, encountering at various times of the night the customary Pacific Ocean turbulence, the great cones of air and cloud which could rise higher than the track of a 747. Tiredness, light-headedness and the prospect of meeting my girls, Judy and my daughters, in some thirteen hours permitted me to achieve some optimism.

It occurred to me on that flight through darkness and quirky columns of air that there was a novelistic neatness to the tale. During the war, Poldek and others had been utterly dependent on Oskar. By the late 1950s, when he abandoned his wife in Argentina, he became dependent upon them, on men like Zuckermann, Number 585, and Pantirer, Number 205, New Jersey real estate developers who peppered the New Jersey suburbs they would develop with Schindler Streets and Schindler Plazas. They had once been the children and he the father, but then, postwar, he became the promising but perpetually erratic child who could never seem to make a go of anything, and who must have found some of the people he had saved a little tiresomely bourgeois. And so, as I had discovered, after times with them in Israel or California, back he went for a season in Frankfurt, in his poor apartment near the Hauptbahnhof, a zone of garish bars, prostitutes and lost souls. "Ah," his survivors would say in documents I now possessed, "the Herr Direktor hasn't changed."

I was in fact so excited by what I had heard from Poldek and Misia and by the documentation I carried with me—even though it constituted a fraction of the material which would be needed to make the book—that when we came in over the coast and the familiar red roofs of Sydney, and I survived the baggage hall and customs and was met by my wife and two teenage daughters, I told them, "Look, before we go home, can we have a cup of coffee? I've got a wonderful story to tell you. See this briefcase— I'm sorry, I had to leave the one you girls gave me behind, but I left it in a flash suite at the Beverly Wilshire."

My daughters had taken to describing me condescendingly as "a funny old thing," but accepted, and in some cases shared, their parents' enthusiasms. And Sydney is an excellent city for coffee—a boon from considerable immigration from southern Europe. After we gave our order I told them, having caught the bug of hyperbole from Poldek, that I had encountered the most wonderful story imaginable, I didn't know if I could write it, but I was thinking of having a try.

As that black coffee injected me with false wakefulness, I narrated everything. I opened my new briefcase—that was part of the story too—and showed them some of the Schindler documents. It was only later in life that I came to appreciate my wife's acceptance of my projects. Judy was not a cat's paw. She had robust Irish convicts in her background, and her elder brother had flown eighty-four missions before the age of twenty-three over Europe in the Second World War, and been multiply decorated. But it's worth reiterating that she had never seen my profession, as economically perilous as it was, as an odd one. I showed them the list. Judy and the girls were captivated by it, its bureaucratic form, the fact that there were names on it belonging to people I had now met and spoken to at length.

The coffee finished, we drove home. Our house lay above a Sydney beach, unspoiled by promenades, cement or hotels, and the garden was connected to the sand by a little track of about forty or fifty meters. My office was located above this track on the ground floor—it had a desk, bookshelves and a pub snooker table which I had purchased from a group of jovial surfies who had mass-rented the place next door. This would prove to be a perfect surface for the spreading of research documents. I often wrote standing up there, clearing off my pages only for an occasional game of pool. Meanwhile, on the beach below, board riders innocent of old-world malice performed their calm stunts amid crashing waves.

From here I began to make Schindler contacts in Sydney. First was a meeting with a general practitioner, Dr. Roman Rosleigh, who practiced medicine from a surgery at the front of a bungalow in the eastern Sydney suburb of Rose Bay. Rosleigh was a stately, handsome man, a contemporary of Poldek, a survivor of Płaszów and of its evil commandant Amon Goeth. He had been a doctor in the camp hospital and now he was generous with his information. When he first arrived in Australia as what the locals called "a reffo," he had worked in a tire factory until he passed the certification exams the authorities imposed on immigrant doctors. He had founded an Australian family—I would often run into his son at the Sydney Football Stadium, wearing an Easts football sweater, no shadow of evil Płaszów or of Amon Goeth hanging over him. As for Dr. Rosleigh's daughter, Monica, she is now the director of a nuclear medicine department in one of Sydney's hospitals.

Dr. Rosleigh had not been on Oskar's list for Brinnlitz, but he had often observed Schindler as he moved about Płaszów on business and had great respect for him, he said. And he knew intimately many of the *Schindlerjuden*. He'd known Stern, Schindler's chief accountant and reputedly a great influence upon Oskar. He had seen, from his post in the clinic, Amon Goeth striding along or riding his white horse around the interior roads of the Płaszów camp, with each prisoner his eye lit upon feeling doomed to a bullet, if not today then tomorrow. Dead Goeth rampaged through Dr. Rosleigh's dreams as he did through the dreams of all survivors of Płaszów.

As we drank tea in the house after surgery hours, he showed me a treasure from his bookshelf. It was the Polish transcript of Amon Goeth's postwar trial, the full account by witnesses of Goeth's behavior, beginning with the time he rolled into Kraków from Tarnów with the job of liquidating the Kraków ghetto. It covered the random shooting of prisoners from his balcony; the numbers of Polish Gentiles and Jews who were slaughtered at Chujowa Górka, a former Austrian hill fort at the southwestern end of the camp; his ambiguous relationship of hate and desire with his maid Helen Hirsch; his teasing of the boy prisoner Lysiek with the prospect of death, followed by his ultimate delivery of it with a bullet—all this freshly remembered in the evidence of those witnesses who in 1946 brought down a guilty verdict upon Amon's head and sent him to the gallows.

Dr. Rosleigh, short of time, nonetheless patiently took me through the transcript, translating sections into English.

The transcript of the trial was also richly interspersed with photographs, including a photograph of the sensualist Goeth, in a fairly ordinary suit, being hanged from a low scaffold at Płaszów, scene of his crimes.

Dr. Rosleigh had a professional gravitas Poldek lacked, and

to hear the same stories emerging from both kinds of men, so far apart geographically, impressed me greatly. There *had* been a fallible, heavy-drinking man named Schindler who had provided rescue, but he did it by drinking with another fallible yet utterly warped man of the same age, Obersturmführer (First Lieutenant) Amon Goeth.

Poldek had also given me the Sydney address of a family named the Korns, Leosia and Edmund, or Edek. In Brinnlitz, Oskar's second camp in Czechoslovakia, Edek had been a welder with Poldek, and he too had the build I came to associate with male Holocaust survivors—below six feet, a compact trunk with considerable upper body strength or wiriness. Leosia was different—a delicately built woman, like Misia. Also like Misia, she had been on Schindler's list for Brinnlitz, but had found herself by accident, and with the other Schindler women, right in the midst of that very conurbation of slaughter, Auschwitz. How astounding to see her in a pleasant home in the eastern suburbs, where she lived on the incline rising to the sandstone cliffs of Bondi.

When, apparently miraculously after three weeks, Leosia was shipped out of Auschwitz again with the others for Brinnlitz, she weighed less than forty-four kilos, was suffering from scarlet fever and did not have the resistance to combat it. She was put to bed among the boilers in the basement of the Brinnlitz factory, where Mrs. Emilie Schindler hand-fed her semolina she had acquired on the black market. Leosia was able to get out of her cot, in that warm cellar at the end of one of Europe's saddest winters, on the day before the German surrender. Yet there she is on the list, marked down like frail Misia as a *Metallarbeiterin*. There were few other spaces than that boiler room where she could have survived. These grandparents, Edek and Leosia, now took their children and grandchildren to Bondi and were Sydney and eastern suburbs patriots in the same way Poldek was a Beverly Hills patriot.

The Korns' immigration story was a little like Leopold and Misia's. When they arrived in Sydney postwar, they had been amazed to discover that the chief sectarian fight was not between Gentile and Jew but, at that stage, between Catholic and Protestant. "I said to a friend," Leosia told me, "here the Catholics are the Jews!" Australians, who with unabashed xenophobia labeled all foreigners *wogs*, did not discriminate between Polish Catholics and Polish Jews, and abused them both with equal ferocity. Equality at last, thought the Korns.

At first Edek had worked at a rubber factory. In the period immediately after the war, housing was so short in Australia that if you wanted to rent the humblest flat, you were forced to offer the agent and/or owner a special tax named "key money"—that is, a bribe. His fellow workers in the rubber factory, who knew him by now, took up a collection and raised the key money he needed. It was given to him by one of his Australian coworkers with the words, "Listen, you wog bastard. Make sure you pay it all back!" That was the thing about Australians, said Edek Korn, quite admiringly. When you first arrived and they didn't know you or like you they called you a wog bastard, and when they got to know and like you they called you a wog bastard. It was characteristic of a society largely made up of the hard-handed descendants of economic and political refugees that men expressed their deepest prejudice and their truest affection in the same words and with barely altered emphasis.

As soon as they could, Edek and Leosia had acquired some sewing machines, rented an upstairs room in an inner suburb, and started turning out trousers. One thing the Holocaust did for its survivors—and the experience of being a *Schindlerjude* did it too—was to give them vocational flexibility. They would turn their hand to anything that might earn them a space to breathe on earth.

By the time I met them, the Korns were well-to-do manufacturers, but Leosia confessed to me that she could never leave home to go shopping, even to the plush emporium of David Jones in the Central Business District, without taking with her a crust of bread. It was a quirk I would run up against in many of the *Schindlerfrauen*. Reason told them that between Dover Heights and Sydney, between New Jersey and Manhattan, they were unlikely to be loaded unexpectedly into a truck and shipped away, but the experience of hunger was so seared into their brains that they could not travel without the irrational fear that the bus or the taxi in which they rode would be stopped, that the trucks of the tyrant would lie in their paths, that they would be taken off their conveyances and packed tight in something in which there was no guarantee of survival, let alone the next meal. I told this story at a table of survivors in a New York restaurant, and almost shamefully a number of women began to confess they were the same, and took crusts from their handbags to prove it.

The Korns had two daughters, one a mother of young children, and another about to become an eminent criminologist. One took from the Korns a sense of precisely what talent had been redeemed from the furnace, though a mere modicum of the whole tapestry, of course.

I had to go to Melbourne too, and set up a meeting with a family named the Rosners, who lived there. The Rosner brothers had enjoyed the curious privilege of being Amon Goeth's musicians in Płaszów. Before the war, Leo Rosner, an accordionist, had performed in the best hotels in Kraków with his brother Henry, a violinist. Even in the ghetto they were sometimes summoned to Nazi parties, and they played together in cafés inside the ghetto itself. Then, in the Płaszów camp, it was under orders that they put on their dinner suits in the appalling barracks to go up to Goeth's villa and perform at lunches and cocktail parties. They got used to playing on, sustaining the required flow of music no matter what happened in Goeth's living room and on the balcony. Now Leo and Henry did not live on the same continent—Henry lived in Queens, and I hoped to see him eventually.

Since the first discovery of gold near Melbourne, Sydneysiders and Melburnians have been locked in rivalry for a century and a half, and I was amused to find that Leo Rosner, Schindler survivor and accordion player, was a full-throated participant in the dialogue. "You should live in Melbourne," he told me in the Rosner house in the Melbourne suburb of Elsternwick. "We have better roads. Sydney people are so ruthless. Thank God I came to Melbourne!" His intense civic pride was characteristic of Melburnians, who possessed a municipal self-esteem which puts the more relaxed Sydneysiders to shame. In the most congenial way possible, Leo Rosner had survived to become a typical Melburnian. A patriot of that golden city, as Edek Korn was of Sydney and Poldek of his "California, Beverly Hills."

Like Edek Korn, Rosner proved to be a sturdy little man, and was still a professional musician, in demand for weddings and parties all over the state of Victoria, being equally able to play a rousing Australian folk song and a plangent prewar Hungarian song of doomed love. His brother, he told me, regularly played the violin at the Sign of the Dove in New York. "Poldek will take you there," he promised. It was an appropriate idea, because Rosner possessed much of Poldek's own indomitability. But it became apparent, too, that many who possessed these qualities had once, for a second, taken the wrong direction, been stopped with a bullet, or forced to ingest the lethal gas. It was in the women, in his wife, Helena, who had survived the Holocaust without being a Schindler Jew, that one encountered the fragility, the wariness, the gentleness, and the more subtle invincibility.

It was during these visits to the Rosners that I met another Schindler survivor, this time from Argentina, a man named Edward Heuberger, a blithe, sun-tanned, open-browed sort of man who contributed his tale of Płaszów, Schindler's DEF (Emalia) and Brinnlitz. He had been one of the young prisoners who at the war's end had accompanied Oskar to the West, to testify on his behalf should he be captured. They had finally run into an American patrol just beyond the Austrian border.

Heuberger, not having seen any cinema for many years, was astonished by the fact that the Americans all chewed either tobacco or gum in a uniform display of mastication as they took Europe away from the Wehrmacht.

Heuberger gave me a very detailed account of that journey to the West, including the confiscation of Schindler's diamond-loaded Mercedes by the Czech underground, and the ultimate arrest of Schindler by the Allies in Konstanz, near the Swiss border. He was soon freed on the strength of a plea signed by all his prisoners.

Back in Sydney's northern beaches, from the desk in my office, I began composing an account of Schindler's activities, on the basis of a possible contract from Nan Talese. I could see the husky, nonverbal surfers riding their boards on the beach below. The beach we lived on seemed frequently to guarantee good wave formations—*sets*, as the board riders called them.

By December 1980, I took off for Los Angeles again to formalize arrangements and plans for a research journey with Poldek and Glovin, leaving a family who had become enthused with the story by way of our table talk. Nan Talese had offered an advance of U.S.$60,000, not a bad advance by the standards of 1980. It would enable me to deal with Glovin and to take Poldek with me on a research journey, but also to have a living wage while I wrote the book. My British agent, a splendid woman and by birth an Austrian baroness, Tessa Sayle (formerly von Stockert), took the treatment and the abstract and showed them to a British publisher called Hodder & Stoughton, particularly to a jolly, bearded editor named Ion

Trewin. So Hodder & Stoughton, too, became interested in the book for English and Australian publication, and at some stage gave me an advance for it.

I was suddenly in deep. It was where, to be honest, I wanted to be. There was a hunger for more tales of simultaneous horror and deliverance. I did not pause to ask what that said of my nature. Writers don't.

With Poldek in 1981 at 48 Grodzka Street, his old home in Kraków, where his mother ran her interior decorating business.

At Schindler's grave in Jerusalem, 1981.

With Judy at Schindler's plaque on the "Avenue of the Righteous," Jerusalem, 1981. (Note the briefcase purchased from Poldek.)

Tom at the entrance of Auschwitz 1 in 1981. (The top of the gate reads, "Work makes you free.")

Tom with Henry Rosner, the New York—based violinist, 1981.

Poldek with child survivor Ryszard Horowitz, who went on to become a brilliant photographer.

Lewis (Lutek) Fagen and his wife, who ran a wholesale business in New York's diamond district. In Brinnlitz, Lutek was charged by the head of the SS garrison with sabotaging a calibrated metal press. Schindler laughed the charge off.

Poldek and Misia with Tom and Jane Keneally at the Keneally family home in Sydney, 1987.

Judy and Margaret Keneally gave Tom a special homecoming at Sydney Airport after *Schindler's Ark* was announced as the winner of the 1982 Booker Prize. The T-shirts were made by family friend Iain Finlay.

(Left to right) Judy, Poldek, Misia, Jane and Tom at a Labor Party lunch at the Regent Hotel in Sydney, where they were to meet up with Bob Hawke. This was Poldek's first and last visit to Australia, in 1987.

An informal meeting on the set of
Schindler's List. (Left to right) Jane Keneally,
Tom, Bonnie Curtis (Spielberg's assistant),
Steven Spielberg, Jerry Molen (producer),
Kathleen Kennedy (producer).

Ben Kingsley and Steven Spielberg on the set of
the re-created Płaszów camp.

Jane and Tom Keneally on set with the
intense Ralph Fiennes.

Vintage trains used to re-create scenes of the
shipment of Jews to the labor camps. These
scenes were particularly difficult for survivors
to watch.

Judy, Tom and Steven Spielberg after the New York premiere of *Schindler's List*.

Meeting the Austrian chancellor, Frank Vranitzky (head of table): Steven Spielberg, Jerry Molen and Tom, February 1994. BELOW: Press conference prior to the film premiere of *Schindler's List* in Vienna, February 1994. (Left to right) Jerry Molen, Tom, Steven Spielberg, Simon Wiesenthal (war-criminal hunter) and Branko Lustig (producer and child survivor of Auschwitz).

Simon Wiesenthal, Spielberg, Tom and Poldek with the U.S. ambassador to Vienna, Swanee Grace Hunt, at a party she hosted at the U.S. embassy before the premiere of the film in Vienna, February 1994.

Tom and Poldek were awarded a chocolate Oscar at a pre–Academy Awards party hosted by Century City magnate Joe Segal. They are pictured here with Segal's Australian-born wife, Kaye Kimberly-Clark.

Misia, Poldek, Judy and Tom at the Segal party.

Liam Neeson with Tom at Segal's opulent home. Neeson returned from the bathroom and said to Tom, "The fookin' Cézannes, man! Have you seen the fookin' Cézannes?"

Liam Neeson and Ralph Fiennes ham it up at the Segal party.

Tom and Judy Keneally on their way to the Academy Awards on March 22, 1994, in a stretch limousine arranged for by Universal Studios.

Outside the Academy Awards before the announcement that *Schindler's List* had won Best Film and Spielberg Best Director.

Tom with Ben Kingsley (now Sir Ben Kingsley), who played Itzhak Stern, at the premiere of *Schindler's List* in Sydney.

Three

In California, Poldek was waiting at the airport. "Tow-mass, my brother! We are brothers to the grafe. What a great little guy!"

I could later joke about his grammatical usage, but even here I am partly uneasy for I, too, had a sense we were somehow brother-adventurers, a sense that this journey was somehow larger than the accumulation of our joint endeavors, and a certainty that his Polish was splendid and mine nonexistent.

In the following days I was taken to see more people who had known Schindler—for example, the impressive Rabbi Jacob Pressman in whose temple, Beth Am, Schindler had been a guest and once made a speech. With Irving Glovin in his Glenwood office, I, foolishly perhaps, let loose the fact that I had not knowingly met a Jewish Australian until I was in my twenties. Indeed I confessed that although the Australian forces in World War I had been commanded by the brilliant son of Prussian Jews, General Sir John Monash, after whom an

Australian university and suburbs were named, it was not until my twenties that I caught on to the idea that Monash was actually Monasch. This confession of mine seemed to increase
rather than diminish a certain uneasiness in Glovin about
Poldek's enthusiasm for me.

Amid the visits and extraordinary interviews with Holocaust survivors and Oskar acquaintances, Poldek and Misia
maintained, from their untroubled childhoods, the practice of
giving guests high Polish tea. Resplendent pastries were ar-
rayed in the Pfefferberg apartment in Elm Drive, Beverly
Hills. The walls were covered with scenes of Polish farm-
houses and snowbound streets in Kraków, and paintings of
Hasidic dancers.

Such stories Poldek told, such legends he spun, such good
oil he exuded! Misia too, with softly muttered and extraordinary tales of her time in the presence of Amon Goeth or in
Auschwitz, holding her breath, barely possessing the strength
to stand, rubbing beets into her face to put color in her cheeks
as the bored, sardonic SS doctors went by, selecting. I knew,
even then, that I would try to write the book in the spirit of
Tom Wolfe, as what Truman Capote or his publisher called *fac-
tion*. I knew, too, that things said by any one interviewee would
have to be matched or weighed against what the historic record
said, against context and the memories of other former
Schindlerjuden.

One early story Poldek told me again, but not in Misia's
hearing, concerned the requirement laid down by the SS for
delousing plants in all their camps, including Schindler's. The

sons-of-bitch Nazis, he said, as willing as they were for Jews to suffer from typhus, were very particular about its power to disrupt production and, above all, to infect them. The mother camp, Gross-Rosen up in Lower Silesia, of which Brinnlitz was a satellite, had ordered Oskar to build one in his factory-camp. Having described himself as a welder for the sake of getting into Brinnlitz, Poldek had to work with Edek Korn, the man I had met in Sydney, in welding a delousing system for prison clothing, blankets and other sources of lice-borne infection. The welders worked day and night on it, because they were anxious that the camp and factory would be closed down by the SS engineers at Gross-Rosen for lack of proper facilities.

After an all-night work session, Poldek claimed, with snow outside the compound and considerable heat in the factory, and with the oxyacetylene dazzling the air, he and Edek decided to ascend to the catwalks which ran across the roof of the factory, and go to one of the water tanks located up there for a quick swim. Upon arrival they found Schindler and a good-looking SS woman sharing the water. In fact, *cavorting* was the word for it. Poseidon and Amphitrite in their heaven. "I said, Forgive me, Herr Direktor! And Edek and I walked away. The Herr Direktor didn't seem to be too worried, he didn't blush. And as long as he was saving us from sons-of-bitch, we were happy. Let him have more girls than King Solomon!"

Further documents were forthcoming now—the entire contents of the filing cabinets at the back of the repair room were photocopied, including the awful SS telegram from Gross-Rosen which arrived at Brinnlitz on the morning of April 28,

1945, addressed not to Oskar but to the SS commandant, Untersturmführer (Second Lieutenant) Liepold, whose job was to guard Schindler's camp. Liepold was ordered to liquidate the prison, and the term "liquidate" meant killing the prisoners. A brave young prisoner named Mietek Pemper, Oskar's secretary, who throughout the war made copies of many such incriminating documents, had a copy of the telegram in Schindler's hands before breakfast time. This day was Schindler's birthday—as early as this, he was already drinking cognac!—and he gave Pemper reassurances of the inmates' survival.

As we went round Los Angeles together, Poldek mentioned off-handedly that he had recently had a heart bypass operation. They weren't as common then as they are at the time of writing, but he told me his cardiac surgeon had declared it necessary, and he had cried, "Let's do it now and get it over." I was astonished that such a vital, hectic man should have recently needed a heart operation, and one at that stage considered quite serious.

He told me, too—not as a related incident but as another stanza of his life as a prisoner—about the SS noncommissioned officer (NCO) who regularly beat him with a truncheon in the barracks at Płaszów. Poldek had somehow attracted the young man's irritable attention. The SS man intended to break Poldek. During one beating Poldek felt a sudden collapse of a disc in his back. But the intuition came to him that if he yelled now, the man would kill him. So he remained silent as his brain shrieked with pain. The beating ended and, from that

point on, the NCO never touched him again, and Poldek became what Himmler had warned the SS about—he became the
man's special friend. As Płaszów was being closed down, the
NCO came to Poldek one night, gave him a bottle of vodka and
advised him to get onto Schindler's list. Then he broke down
and wept and said he had done things his mother wouldn't believe. He hoped to be transferred to the Waffen-SS and die in
battle. As far as Poldek knew, that was what happened, for the
man never turned up on the lists of war criminals and was not
in the files of the Simon Wiesenthal Center.

Poldek and I arranged to begin our research journey to interview survivors and collect documentation in late February.
In the meantime he and I would work on a list of contacts and
their addresses. One of them was Oskar's abandoned wife,
Emilie, in Buenos Aires.

At home on the beach in Sydney, I began to write as much as
I could, basing the text on the documents Poldek had given me
before Christmas and on interviews and documents I had gar-
nered since. I had also collected a set of helpful reference
books on the Holocaust. They included Lucy Davidowicz's history *The War Against the Jews: 1933–1945*; Nora Levin's *The Holocaust*; Raul Hilberg's encyclopedic *The Destruction of the
European Jews*, rich with Nazi documentation; Walter Laqueur's
The Terrible Secret; *Patterns of Jewish Leadership in Nazi Europe,
1933–1945*, the proceedings of a Yad Vashem history conference; the transcript of the trial of Amon Goeth; Martin
Gilbert's *Atlas of the Holocaust* and *Auschwitz and the Allies*; innumerable other books, including the startling biography of

the SS chemical officer Kurt Gerstein, who both supplied Zyklon B to the system yet tried to let the West know about the extermination process—Saul Friedländer's *Counterfeit Nazi*.

In those pre-email days, I made contact with some survivors by letter, including Mietek Pemper, Oskar's former secretary, and Moshe Bejski, an Israeli Supreme Court judge who had once been Oskar's forger of official papers.

I had also already written to Emilie Schindler in Buenos Aires via her lawyer, Juan Caro, whose address Poldek had given me. Oskar's wronged wife, a hero in her own right, lived in San Vicente, a suburb of the city. Poldek had told me there was a devoted group of Argentinian survivors and others in the Jewish community who had sustained Mrs. Schindler in modest comfort since the nutria farm she and Oskar had started went bust in the late 1950s. Juan Caro replied that Mrs. Schindler was ill, too ill to be pestered by a visit. But she would send me answers if I forwarded questions, and I should also forward an appropriate fee at the same time. So I sent off a list of questions, and the substantial fee, to Emilie.

I did not quite understand then that Oskar's abandonment of her was an act of treachery—in fact, the chief treachery she had suffered in her life—and that to hear Oskar praised as heroic, when he had failed to rescue her from the ignominy of being a dumped wife, was for her still the main issue, the unresolved wound, of Schindler's history. In my questions I asked her to describe as fully as she chose the background she and Oskar came from, the circumstances of their marriage, and her own part in any of his activities. I told her that I had already heard tales of her own independent bravery, of her hand-feeding of women such as Leosia Korn. I said I sought to give her a proper place in the book.

She answered these questions perhaps reluctantly but fairly fully. She and Oskar came from the neighborhood of Zwittau (Svitavy) in northeastern Czechoslovakia, an ethnic German town near Brinnlitz, where Oskar would ultimately have his second camp. She did not express in her answers any rancor toward him for the hard dance he had led her through history. She told me particularly of the moribund women like Leosia and Misia, who were extricated from Auschwitz and brought back to Brinnlitz, and then the horrifying story of the two railway carriages that were dumped in the local railway depot at Brinnlitz. They had turned up there in the midst of the war's last savage winter.

I had already heard of these trucks from Poldek and Edek Korn, who were both summoned to cut the frozen locks open. Inside each truck lay a pyramid of dying and dead workers from the Auschwitz quarry of Goleszów. These trucks had been shunted around Eastern Europe for two weeks in that frightful winter.

Frau Schindler's answers did not claim, as some of her friends later did, that she was the chief force behind Oskar's decency toward his Jewish workers. Yet they show she was her own woman and, from Brinnlitz, organized the sale of black-market items to buy food and medicine for both the women who came to her from Auschwitz and for the Goleszów men. Her service to those people was, according to the other prison-

ers, astonishingly generous and full-blooded, and much more
than she would have needed to do to escape any future criminal judgment should this happen to be the war's last autumn
and winter.

The contract from Simon & Schuster arrived, and I signed
it on the pool table among the Schindleriana I had so far collected, and sent it back.

February 1981 came quickly. The beach below our house was
dotted with people, some days crowded with them. My daughters went swimming and watched Australia play a Test series
against New Zealand on television. It is a good, lazy month in
Sydney, with the new school year just begun.

Back across the Pacific again, the lights of Sydney soon lost,
there was nothing to see until, with morning and sunshine
falling on Catalina Island off one wing, we inserted ourselves
into the great air jam around Los Angeles airport.

There was time for a last few interviews in Los Angeles before Poldek and I took to our journey. I now met a middle-aged
woman, a radio journalist and survivor who made a particular
point to me. She insisted that she was one of Schindler's Jews
too, even though she hadn't been to Brinnlitz. She was a
Schindler Jew, she said, in the sense that the Czechoslovakian
province of Moravia had been kept free of Jewish labor camps
for nearly five years of the war. It was the Reich's concession to
the wishes of the local Sudeten German population, and it was
also the wish of the Moravian police chief, Otto Rasch. The
prisoners all seemed to take it for granted that Schindler had

offered inducements to Rasch to persuade him to permit the opening of his labor camp in the province. Once the precedent had been created, there was room for other camps.

According to this woman, many young Jews whose lives would have been lost one way or another in the liquidation of Auschwitz, as the Russian army drew near the Vistula and the German factories were moved out of Auschwitz-Monowitz, were now sent to labor in a sequence of new Moravian work camps. This woman, very Californian, well-coiffed, expensively dressed, told me that she had been a prisoner in a Luftwaffe manufacturing plant in Moravia that would never have been opened had Schindler not broken the ground first by founding his own plant. Later I read the same argument in some documents written by Oskar's accountant Itzhak Stern, and supplied to me by his widow. Itzhak would make the claim that up to twenty thousand Jewish prisoners were saved by Oskar's initiative in Moravia.

As well as introducing me to Holocaust survivors in the 1939 Club—a Beverly Hills survivors' club Poldek had helped found, whose members had not necessarily been in Oskar's camp but who had known him postwar in California and Israel—Poldek talked to me endlessly about Goeth and Oskar and the SS and prisoners he knew, and answered my questions. I made notes on paper or by tape recorder. On the streets of Beverly Hills, his flow was interrupted only by ornate nods to friends or conversations with them, many being either former prisoners or people who had met Oskar or both.

In Gelson's Supermarket in Beverly Hills on a Sunday morning, he stopped suddenly in front of the fruit section like a man struck by an intuition and reached out his hand to an elderly woman who seemed to be considering buying a melon. "Janka, darling. How did you get even more beautiful than to start with?" They kissed each other on both cheeks, Eastern European style, and Leopold introduced me. "Yes, there is going to be a book, darling. And a film. Sure, this will be a film. Why wouldn't it be? Such a story of humanity man to man," etc., etc., After asking her to raise her chin and proclaiming "Ageless, darling! Such bone structure!" a number of times, and making kissing sounds, he bade the woman good-bye, completed his purchases, and led me back to his car.

Apart from the fact that the woman was magnificent despite her years, Poldek's flattery worked not because it was mere flattery. He believed his own exuberant claims. To him, beauty was a regularly encountered commodity.

"Do you know," he asked me, "that gorgeous woman killed the son-of-bitch *Gauleiter* of Riga?" The *Gauleiter* were the provincial governors of the Reich. "She was living on Aryan papers. Seduced the son-of-bitch, and let the underground into the bedroom to finish him! Such a looker!"

This question of "Aryan papers" would arise again and again. Young middle-class Jewish women were generally the ones who had used this stratagem of obtaining by whatever means, money or charm, fake papers that declared them *Volksdeutsche*—ethnic Germans—or at least Gentile Poles. There were women still in Europe, Leopold believed, who had never come out after the war from the deep cover of their Aryan identity. "Why should they," Poldek asked, "the way they were hated in Europe?" Some men had done so as well, but it was harder for men—if you were circumcised and pretending to be an Aryan, you needed a certificate that said doctors had been forced to circumcise you because of your having contracted gonorrhea.

I was becoming aware that many Jewish survivors believed, rightly or wrongly, that the Nazis placed so many concentration camps in Poland because of the ripe streak of anti-Semitism in its Catholic community. But Poldek did not make any assertions of that kind. He had remained a Polish nationalist in the Kościuszko tradition, to an extent which annoyed some of his fellow survivors. He was a patriotic supporter of Polish Solidarity, loved Lech Wałęsa, and supplied food packages to a number of Solidarity families via a packager in Chicago. He was also outrageously proud of "the Polish Pope," a pope who made many Catholics I knew—indeed, many clergy—uneasy, and who seemed to be steering the Church back to the doctrinal severity and legalism which had prevailed before the Second Vatican Council and John XXIII.

"I was commissioned an officer in the Polish army," he told me, "in the Rynek of Warsaw in 1938 by Marshal Piłsudski himself." He had also completed his physical education degree at the Jagiellonian University in Kraków, for which he had a passionate love, boasting of its massive history—it had been founded in 1364. "Beside the Jagiellonian," he chuckled, "Yale and Harvard are juniors, nothing but *boychickels*." Yet when he attended there, in Piłsudski's Poland, the university featured a number of well-placed benches on which Jews were not permitted to sit.

Four

Flying by night to save time, Poldek and I arrived in New York with a long list of interviewees to cover, all of whom had no need to cooperate except on Poldek's say-so. The city's freezing air seemed the polar opposite of the sweltering Australian February, and yet felt more appropriate for research purposes of this nature. It was less beach-crazed than Sydney, less airheaded than Los Angeles, and in this weather I didn't need, for example, to plot a time in the day when I could go swimming.

In the Diamond District of New York, on an upper floor of a building right on the corner of Fifth Avenue and Forty-seventh Street, a family of Schindler survivors now named the Fagens (Feigenbaums, as they appear on Schindler's list) ran a splendid wholesale diamond and jewelry business. The Diamond District was and always would be intriguing to me, with its lines of retail jewelers at street level and wholesalers like the Fagens on the floors above, and every potential design to be had. I had from some obscure genetic gift a love of jewelry, one ever restricted by lack of means. I had in my time bought nearly all the jewelry my wife and daughters said they needed, and sometimes items they didn't. Yet I wore none myself. I came from a painfully unflamboyant Australian male tradition.

On Forty-seventh Street I was fascinated to see Hasidic Jews in their black hats moving about the streets, selling the retailers diamonds they had taken on consignment. It seemed to me that in dangerous New York the Hasidim were exceptionally safe traveling around with their pocketed diamonds, and this was a mystery I thought I might one day enquire into. Perhaps understandably, I never quite got the full tale of the relationship between upstairs, the Hasidim, and the street-level stores. Even these days, though the Diamond District website acknowledges the place of the Hasidim, their precise role is not explained.

Upstairs, admitted to the Fagens' office via electronic doors, I met the younger Fagen, Lewis, or—as Poldek called him—Lutek, a slim, likeable fellow, elegantly dressed, who had spent part of his childhood and adolescence in Schindler's two camps. His parents, Necha and Jakob, were also on the list, and his cancer-stricken sister was taken along to Brinnlitz too, and died there in humane dignity, safe from molestation.

On the list in Schindler's Brinnlitz camp, Lutek Fagen was described as capable of working a lathe and of calibrating, but the machine he labored at confounded him. Fagen was charged by the head of the SS garrison, Untersturmführer Liepold, with sabotaging a calibrated metal press. Schindler had laughed the matter off—"striking me over the face, to save my life. I had two kinds of tears in my eyes. Gratitude and because he was strong." He then fobbed Liepold off with some blather or other about how they were all incompetent but could not all be shot.

One of the most important aspects of his imprisonment involved Mrs. Schindler. He had broken his glasses on the factory floor, and Emilie Schindler had said, "Give them to me, and next time I'm up in Kraków, I'll go and see your eye doctor and have them made up again to prescription." This had been a salient moment for Lutek. Here was a boy who, ever since reaching adolescence, had been by decree a subhuman, an *Untermensch*. And yet a Sudeten German woman was willing to recognize him as a young man with a history of prescription glasses, and give him the dignity of a replacement pair. While the SS had heaped up the confiscated lenses and frames of Europe's Jews, dissenters, gypsies and other innocents, Mrs. Schindler was willing to supply at least one set of spectacles to counterbalance a little the pyramids of general confiscation. She would also appear at the side of his sister, as she was dying of cancer, with what seemed to be a miraculous midwinter gift—an apple. Understandably enough, Emilie had not mentioned either of these gifts in her replies to my questions. For Fagen, they constituted one of the major humane gestures of his war. For her it was all probably lost among the memories of more conspicuous favors done.

One night in New York, soon after meeting Lutek and then his elegant, stylish wife, we traveled on the frequently unreliable evening commuter train to Long Island with a New York engineer, a former Holocaust survivor who had married Oskar's mistress Ingrid. This man had survived Mauthausen and then a death march of prisoners to the west. Escaping the line one day, reaching a fringe of trees and finding a farmhouse ahead, he was caught in a barn by a young SS man who had been sent after him. The young soldier, one of the less than utterly Hitlerite conscripts the SS had had to fall back upon in the last months of the Reich, said to him, "The war's nearly over and it's too late for me to start killing people. Make damn sure you lie low here for a long time after we've gone." And with that he went outside and discharged his rifle into the air, and walked off to rejoin the death column. Many of the friends of the *Schindlerjuden* were saved by such individual acts of clemency, though a vaster number were not.

When we got to the engineer's prosperous suburban bungalow on Long Island, I was fascinated to meet his wife, whom so many prisoners had mentioned as a kindly and cooperative presence. Oskar had had an ongoing affair with her all through his years in Kraków, and took her south with him to his new camp, even though it was located on the home turf of Emilie Schindler, and Emilie lived with Oskar in his quarters, an arrangement that had not prevailed in Kraków. Even after the war, when he had fled to Munich, Oskar's household consisted of himself, Emilie and Ingrid. Ingrid's husband, this Jewish man who had survived the Mauthausen death march on the moral whim of an SS conscript and also fetched up in Munich, had met Oskar and his ménage, and he claimed that one night

Oskar had said to him, "Why don't you marry Ingrid? Emilie's getting sick of this arrangement."

Since everyone seemed to do what Oskar wanted in the end, Ingrid *did* eventually marry the former prisoner, quite a departure for the strapping Aryan girl who had been Oskar's helpmeet. She was now a very generous but nervous grandmother. She had prepared a Polish meal for us, but was anxious, by the time I met her, lest her children and grandchildren should hear too much concerning her liaison with the racy Oskar Schindler. That is why I still use "Ingrid" as a pseudonym for her.

Interestingly, this couple had also played a considerable part in Emilie's life, and had kept in contact to the extent that later, when Emilie visited New York, she stayed with them. It was as if Oskar's intentions, not always honorable, had been rendered benign by the parties themselves.

In New York in particular, under the aegis of Uncle Poldek, I began to encounter my first *Schindlerkinder*, children who had an association with the huge, bluff Aryan Oskar. It became apparent immediately that the children had been the most deeply marked and haunted by the war. I met a highly successful former child victim, Ryszard Horowitz, one of the youngest survivors of Auschwitz, at his studio in Manhattan. After the war, before the family moved to America, he had graduated from the Academy of Fine Art in Kraków, along with his childhood friend, Roman Polanski. "The most important heritage I got from my country," he once said of Poland, "is an understanding of art, painting in particular."

His surreal and vivid pictures show a great hunger for pushing at the walls of the normal, three-dimensional world, to make fantastic escapes. One might glibly think that this is his triumph over the savage walls placed around his freedom in childhood. In any case, Ryszard emerged as one of the great photographers of this age. Again, one could look at his open, well-tanned yet profoundly private face and wonder what it was about him as an infant that the Reich should try to kill him.

Even to please Uncle Poldek, it was difficult for him to speak about his memories of the process to which his family and he had been subjected. He left one in no doubt that he believed his daily existence had been cramped and limited by that savage experience, by the merciless flux during which people in whom you made a hopeful investment of love vanished almost at once without explanation or, again without explanation, were butchered in front of you.

Gradually we met other members of Ryszard's family who were also *Schindlerjuden*: his parents, Regina and Dolek Horowitz, and his aunt and uncle, Manci and Henry Rosner. Regina and Manci were sisters, while Henry's brother was the Melbourne accordionist Leo Rosner, mentioned earlier. The Horowitzes were welded to the Rosners by marriage, by the sociability of the parents, and by shared grief and peril. And so we met the other of Amon Goeth's camp musicians, Henry Rosner, compact and jolly, with impish eyes, the violinist from Queens who these days catered to a less lethal clientele at the Sign of the Dove.

Henry's wife, Manci, was impressively articulate, and her robust capacity to talk about the past helped vastly. Even in the moment of their redemption she and Regina suffered an astounding sorrow. Taken out of the slaughter yards of Auschwitz with all the other Schindler women, and awaiting a train to Brinnlitz in the Auschwitz railway concourse, the sisters spotted young Ryszard Horowitz, Regina's son, and his older cousin, Olek (Alec), Manci's cherished boy, waving to their mothers from behind the wire of the men's compound. Both these children were meant to be in Brinnlitz with their fathers! The women hid under a truck to talk to them. "What are you doing here, little darlings?" they called.

It had happened that on one occasion when Oskar was absent from Brinnlitz, the toddler Ryszard was seen playing on the factory floor by an SS inspector on a visit from Gross-Rosen camp. Ryszard was gathered for shipment to Auschwitz with his cousin Olek, who was discovered in the prisoners' quarters. Both their fathers, Dolek Horowitz and Henry Rosner the violinist, volunteered to go with them. They traveled under guard by passenger train, and were amazed at the strained looks on the other passengers' faces, by which they interpreted the war to be going well for the Allies. Then, on arrival at Auschwitz, they were all given the tattoo, meaning they were saved from immediate extinction. The boys proudly displayed their tattoos to the women under the trucks. Then the women were forced by guards to board and to leave their children behind, believing them consigned to death now.

For most child survivors the horror of childhood hung over all the connections and potential happiness of adult life. Ryszard's cousin Olek, a successful sound engineer who owned his own company, the former little boy who hid in the

pit of a latrine to escape a *Hilfsaktion* (health selection) in
Płaszów, reiterated the same idea: "We grew up not trusting
anyone. No sooner did we become attached to someone than
they were taken from us. Even our fathers were taken from us,
when we were moved to the children's huts in Auschwitz 1."
The young fathers nevertheless survived the war, being ordered to labor in Auschwitz 2 rather than sent to the gas
chambers.

After the war, the Red Cross and UNRRA (the United Nations Relief and Rehabilitation Administration) were able to
reunite Olek with his parents, the Rosners, but could provide
no information about Ryszard for the Horowitzes. Regina
Horowitz was watching a newsreel of the liberation of Auschwitz
in a Kraków cinema when she saw Ryszard (in footage destined
to appear in every documentary on Auschwitz) being shunted by
a Polish nun along the wire of Auschwitz 1 toward the gate. "He's
alive," she screamed. She was forced to leave the cinema, but
Ryszard was found.

Questions such as how the boys felt when their mothers
steamed out of Auschwitz—having no choice, of course, but
children don't necessarily understand that—were too grievous
to ask either of these men, Ryszard and Olek. But generally,
Poldek was willing to be insistent that people *must* give us an
interview. He called another couple who lived on Long Island.
The wife had been a sprinter who represented Poland in the
1936 Olympic Games in Berlin, and then, some seven years
later, found herself running up and down the muddy *Appellplatz* (parade ground) in Płaszów to prove that she had not broken down and was not yet ready for obliteration.

I could well understand that these people who had once been *Untermenschen* by decree would not now wish to revisit those times for the sake of a supposed writer (non-Jewish) from the Antipodes who was going to re-create their stories. There were two questions they could ask: (1) What will he understand anyhow, whatever I tell him? (2) Why should I go back to those times for the convenience of some writer? Poldek neither encouraged nor permitted such refusals, though.

"Thomas and I are in New York just two more days," he said to the Long Island couple, the Kinstlingers, "and we can interview you at seven-thirty tomorrow night."

They responded, "Poldek, we have a dinner to go to."

It was no doubt the truth. But Poldek said, "So Schindler saves your life and you don't care enough to cancel a lousy dinner engagement? Is this what I'm to tell Pemper in Munich? And Bejski in Israel?"

That was how I met the former sprinter and her husband—indeed, some days after the interview, on our last night in New York, Poldek insisted that before flying to Europe we visit their generous table and dine copiously on Polish food. Again, Poldek's rule was never to approach any flight unless well-fed. "Those airlines," he gurgled, urging me to clean my plate, "they serve cardboard."

Mr. Kinstlinger had a less fraternal attitude to Herr Direktor Schindler than Poldek, the Rosners, Ingrid and her family, the Horowitz family and other New York area *Schindlerjuden* I interviewed.

"Look, he made plenty out of us, that guy."

"But he saved you, Henry."

"Yeah, yeah. It suited him to let us breathe. But he made plenty out of us. He was no saint."

"Would you rather he was son-of-bitch, starving and beating us?"

"Okay, he didn't starve, he didn't beat. But he used us."

"What makes you bitter?" Poldek challenged him.

"I'm not bitter, but I tell you, he made plenty."

"And lost it all!"

"That's not our fault."

I already felt as glutted with stories as I was with Polish pierogis, but there were many, many miles to travel yet and a night flight to endure. We found ourselves after midnight queuing at JFK for a Lufthansa flight to Frankfurt, as a base from which we could meet up with Oskar's former secretary Mietek Pemper and others. A young Hasidic Jew was moving down the line of passengers as we waited to embark—a not uncommon practice in New York, where the Hasid chooses a person who looks like a worldly Jew and urges him to lead a more Orthodox life. To my astonishment, the young Hasid stopped in front of me.

"Excuse me, sir," he said very politely, "are you Jewish?"

Poldek, unabashed in a queue which included many Germans, roared, "No! I'm the Jew. He's an Australian, you schmuck!"

The line reverberated through the departure hall, and so we boarded.

Five

Thanks to the destruction of the old city in World War II, Frankfurt am Main proved to be a fairly anonymous place full of modernist architecture. It had a nickname to go with its look—Mainhattan. There were not many *Schindlerjuden* in Frankfurt, but the one I remembered best was Adam Garde (Number 656), who lived with his wife in a small but superbly designed Frankfurt apartment. Garde's hand had been crushed, as he now showed me, when he was building Goeth's conservatory in Płaszów. For fear of being sent away to a death camp because of his disabling injury, he had to conceal the damage. Though one of the Jewish doctors in Płaszów put it in a cast, he cut it free for fear he might be shipped out. He was delighted to go to work in Oskar's factory, DEF, in Kraków, and to land in Oskar's camp in the enamel factory backyard. As a result of that, he went on to Oskar's new camp in Brinnlitz.

An engineer, Garde had stayed on in Germany after being released from a displaced persons' camp, and had a positive view of German society. Unlike many of his fellow survivors in other places, he considered Nazism something that could happen anywhere, the result of a failure of civilization, a disease in the universal soul rather than a phenomenon specific to Germany.

He told me about his experiences of being one of Oskar's engineers. He assured me that in both Emalia and Brinnlitz, Schindler would have him subtly decalibrate machines, so that the production tests of shells would fail. He was not the only one to tell me that to pass a test late in the war, Oskar ordered in a supply of shells from another manufacturer. With all the complaints coming in from other factories about the deficiency of the shells Oskar was making, the prisoners themselves would have wanted the factory at Brinnlitz to have a good reputation so that it could continue as their haven. It was Oskar who took joy in flouting the system, not his engineers like Garde. And it was Oskar who, drinking cognac on the morning of his birthday, laughed off a telegram from an assembly factory complaining about the poor quality of the shell casings Brinnlitz produced.

In Germany, Poldek's energy remained ferocious. After the city's Historisches Museum and Jüdisches Museum, we visited the central railway station, the Hauptbahnhof, an ambiguous place full of lost souls and garish bars. Walking north from the station, past strip joints and more bars, we came to the decaying nineteenth-century facade of the apartment building to which Oskar always returned from his adventures in America or Israel, as if to recover from the respectability of those whom he had saved. The place possessed a piss-reeking lobby and seedy grand stairway. But it was from here, long after the war, that Oskar pursued his last love affair, this one with a German surgeon's wife. He had first spoken to this lover, Anne-Marie, in the King David Hotel during one of his Israel visits. And it was here in his apartment on an upper floor that Oskar, a strange kind of displaced person himself, sneered at by anti-Semites and closet Hitlerites, had collapsed in October 1974, and was taken to the hospital where he died on October 9.

All our touring and research was considered by Poldek to be a mere prelude to meeting the former secretary Mietek Pemper, who lived and worked as an accountant in Munich. Yet even on the plane journey down there, sitting side by side, Poldek instructed and I wrote. What I had heard from people kept me wakeful. I was full of the chemicals which guarantee industry. A parallel force in me kept me writing, writing, and Poldek talking, talking.

At the airport in Munich we were met by the sober, reticent, learned Mietek Pemper, the man who had been secretary to Amon Goeth, commandant of Płaszów, as well as to Oskar Schindler. At the risk of his life but for the sake of history, and for ultimate evidence against Amon, he had always made an extra carbon copy of camp documents, and hidden that copy, or passed it to Schindler. The SS, who looked toward the completion of their plan and the disappearance of a race, did not take into account the Pempers, for in their belief Pemper was scheduled to disappear too.

Temperamentally, Mietek Pemper still seemed to possess some of the august loneliness which must have attached to his secret garnering of carbon copies of Goeth's correspondence. It became obvious to me as he took us to his black Mercedes in the airport car park that if Poldek ever revered anyone, it was this man. Pemper took us to the Bavarian Provincial Museum and introduced me to some significant documents on the SS. I had a feeling he was testing me, to see if I were the right person and could make use of resources. There was a tendency on the part of some of the survivors, when during a meeting Poldek would leave for a moment, to warn me to be careful of Poldek's exuberant narratives. They were worried in case something unreliable was published. I believed that, even given my own enthusiasm, I had to be careful, but they could not know that. When three or four survivors told the same story, though, and the story was supported by documents . . . well, I believed it had just about earned its place in the ultimate record.

Scholarly Pemper either agreed or asked to read the manuscript when it was done—his manner made it hard to distinguish an offer from a demand. In any case, he would be able to sort out its excesses and errors, and I was very pleased that he was willing to do so. It was an offer-cum-demand that many other survivors would also quite rightly make, but the validity of their requests meant that this book would be all the more in the tradition of Capote and the early Tom Wolfe.

At our hotel that evening, after interviewing Pemper,

Poldek showed me a fairly nondescript badge. With pride, he said, "I bought this for two hundred dollars in New York."

"Two hundred dollars? Is it a special badge?"

"*Is it a special badge?*" he repeated in affectionate mimicry. "I'm telling you, it's the official badge of Orbis, the Polish government's travel agency. It opens doors." His eyes glittered with the hope of the benefits this dourly enameled badge would bring us in Poland.

The next day Pemper showed me a number of his Schindler documents for copying and to add to the record, and then, after he had adequately explained them to me, delivered us back to Munich airport. We caught a slightly seedy LOT Airlines jet and, penetrating steely clouds, it brought us into dismal Poland in early evening. General Jaruzelski, the Polish prime minister, had banned the new people's liberation movement, Solidarity (Solidarność), and was girding his loins to proclaim martial law. He had been under pressure to do so from Marshal Kulikov, Russian Commander-in-Chief of the Warsaw Pact Armies, who had twenty Russian divisions ready to take Poland over should the Kremlin consider that necessary. Soon Russian troops were entering anyhow, since Kulikov had insisted that the two armies, Polish and Soviet, should hold joint spring maneuvers.

At a dimly lit Warsaw airport, customs and immigration men were sullen. Indeed, wariness and hostility would characterize the country. Habitually repressed hunger and anger had brought an ineradicable sadness to faces. There was no spacious atmosphere of welcome for the traveler, and despite the occasional poster of skiers in the Carpathians and of the old town of Warsaw, this was not a country for tourists.

Like all visitors, we were required to make a list of all the money and jewelry we had. We were warned by frowning, armed officials in an unspecified uniform that we must always change our dollars at the state exchanges, and we had to sign a document which bound us to do that and present proof that we had when we departed. So a further document was to be given over to government money exchangers every time we changed our dollars for zloty.

After all the gloom of being processed, it was wonderful when we had reclaimed our bags to march out of the sliding door into the main hall and see a jockeylike, leather-capped man waiting for us and beaming. It was our cab driver Marek, whose family Poldek had been supporting with food packages and money. There were many *dzień dobry*s (hellos) as Poldek, unwilling to be repressed by the times, shouted his raucous greetings and kissed Marek on both cheeks.

"This little guy!" intoned Poldek, taking in his fingers a fold of Marek's cheek. "He's a good Pole. He knows Wałęsa. He's Solidarność. Worked in the same shipyard as Wałęsa!"

Marek revived my spirits by not seeming too scared of Poldek's enthusiasm, though he did make the mildest restraining gesture with his hand. In response, Poldek turned to me and said huskily, "Don't talk loud, Thomas. Better be careful in case some son-of-bitch listens."

Led by Marek, we walked out to where his taxi was parked. He insisted on carrying our heavy bags, but I kept in my hand the briefcase I had bought from Poldek the previous October. By now it contained a trove of interviews, and copies of documents Mietek Pemper had given me. To leave it out of my sight made me restless, so I took it into the backseat of Marek's Mercedes cab. Poldek, in front with Marek, discussed the state of the nation in Polish.

The streets we drove through seemed identically full of Stalinist tenement blocks. Warsaw looked a cheerless city, but Poldek insisted on being cheered despite it all. A homecoming, he told me. *"Polonia!* But Marek tells me there are a lot of Russian soldiers here now."

Marek said something and laughed. Poldek explained the joke: "If you smell, you know, human pee all over the place, it's the Russians. They wash their hands in water closets, and piss on the tiles. They know nothing from bathrooms."

Marek continued to fill Poldek in on the tragedy of Poland. Though a grit of weariness seemed to lie over the entire city, a flame of patriotism warmed these two Poles in a taxi on the way to the Orbis Europejski Hotel near the west bank of the Vistula. Poldek would continue to relay the substance of their talks back to me enthusiastically.

"My friend Marek was up in the north when the shipyard strikes began, and the workers sat on the wharves waving at people going past in cars and trams. *Waving* yet! People haven't waved at each other for years in this country."

I could tell by a scapular hanging from his rearview mirror and the Miraculous Medal welded onto the dashboard that Marek was a Catholic, but Poldek was obviously at one with him in their Polish identity. Unlike many former prisoners, Poldek did not view the Polish decades of misery since 1939 in serves-them-right terms. He saw it for the great tragedy it was.

Before going to our rooms we said good night to Marek, and Poldek conducted a two-way conversation with me and the driver about our plans for the following days. We did not need him that evening, since we were going to the old city, and vehicles were not permitted there.

In the unexpectedly bright lobby of our hotel, the government exchange office stood near the reception desk. The official exchange rate was pegged at some thirty-seven zloty to the U.S. dollar. As Poldek checked us in at full volume, I headed for its grille to change my money. Before I reached it, however, Poldek rushed to me. "Thirty-seven zloty to the dollar? Ridiculous! Son-of-bitch thieves. I can get at least three times that on the street!"

"Black market?" I suggested timorously and in a whisper.

"Don't shout it everywhere, Thomas, my dear friend," he advised me, and then vociferously concluded his sign-in at the reception desk, where the clerk seemed as awed by his Orbis badge as Poldek had predicted. Throughout our journeys in Poland, backing up his general air of self-confidence, the badge gave him immediate, unguessed-at authority with hotel staff, causing a flurry among them. He would then raucously put them at ease, praising their bone structure in Polish before uttering many *bardzo dzię kuję*s (thank you very much). Again this was no mere act, however. This was his singing of the survival of the Poles. He overwhelmed people through his genuine joy, and in praising the harried Polish girls of 1981, he sang the remembered glory of the girls of 1939, Jewish and Catholic, all of them with the coming sword hanging above their dazzling heads.

We would be spending some days in Warsaw, not because we had many survivors to visit there but because it was the center of the lost lives of the *Schindlerjuden*, the big smoke of their youth. It was in its large ghetto that the great uprising occurred. Though in the occupation it had been under different administration than Kraków, it was essential background.

On Hitler's orders, Warsaw had been totally dynamited as a final gesture of cultural punishment before Hitler's troops withdrew. But the old town had been rebuilt from photographs and from Canaletto's famous painting of the city. Indeed, the streets of the old town, an easy walk from the hotel, were still under cash-starved but elegant restoration, and again Poldek took a patriotic joy in this, that a nation plundered by the Germans, and economically and politically oppressed by Stalinism, should find the spirit to rebuild its old graciousness, including the fascinating Royal Castle and the Cathedral of St. John, the Jesuit church. In the town square, the Rynek Starego Miasta, Poldek stood expatiating. People gave him a wide berth. With Solidarność consigned to the shadows, and arrests and beatings of its members by the security police, only a lunatic or a man of power could speak at such high volume. In the end, even Poldek fell silent. He stood still and saluted the

dead of history, to whom this city had contributed untold bat-
talions.

There were a number of restaurants nearby, and Poldek had
me eating soups full of barley and dumplings, and delicious
courses of stuffed tripe, considered offal in richer countries
but presented with artistry and succulence here. We finished
with pancakes and drank Hungarian Bull's Blood wine.

Even though Marshal Pilsudski's Sanacja Party had made an
alliance, after the old man's death in 1935, with the Camp of
National Unity, an anti-Semitic group, Poldek considered
these cobblestones on which he himself had been elevated to
the Polish officer corps to be holy ground. A few years after he
received his commission, Poldek's division began a bitter re-
treat before the invading Germans, from the direction of
Wrocław through Katowice to hold a position at Kraków. The
Germans bypassed Kraków, however, and Poldek's division
scuttered out along the road toward Lwów and along more obscure arteries, beneath predatory dive bombers, to take up a
final position at the San, where he was wounded and lost his
beloved platoon sergeant and was helped to hospital in
Przemyśl, by an NCO. The place was soon overrun by the German army and Poldek, recuperating, became a prisoner. It was
while being transhipped in Kraków from one POW train to another, going west to Germany, that he made his escape home,
catching a Number One tram ten blocks to his parents' place in
Grodzka Street, Kraków.

Poldek felt little martial shame over the defeat of 1939. He
seemed genuinely to believe, as the free world itself came to

believe in 1939, that Poland was being punished for its very gallantry and dash by a cruel totalitarian machine not playing by the rules of gallantry.

When we strolled back from the old town to the less exuberant atmosphere of our hotel, the doorman and everyone in the reception area saluted Poldek's Orbis badge.

Six

During our Warsaw time, as leaden autumn dawns led to days full of ambiguous light under which a frightened populace kept their heads down, Poldek took me, for the sake of my education, to the Pawiak prison. The Pawiak, a series of cellars converted into dim interrogation cells, had housed thousands of captured Polish partisans, Jews masquerading as Aryans, and similar perceived threats to the balance of civilization. There was once a tall structure on top of the cellars, a more conventional prison, but it had been dynamited by the Nazis, and Polish nationalist zeal had not yet been applied to its restoration.

Doomed prisoners' near-last thoughts remained scrawled on the walls of Pawiak, and were interpreted in English in a visitors' guide. Many who were either killed here or were sent on from here to concentration camps were, like Poldek, Poland's most passionate children. Scrawled sentiments such as "Poland is deathless!" were common, as were defiant remarks that it would take more than bullets to defeat the Polish people. The one I remember best, however, was the one that said, "Oh God, how they beat me!"

By now, Marek was back with us and drove us around the old Jewish ghetto, with its present-day dreary apartment blocks, and then across to the Praga side of the Vistula and out into the countryside to buy black-market butter—both from lack of butter in Marek's family and also to illustrate how much better-placed farmers and their families were to withstand food shortages under the present tyranny.

Between Poldek and me, the argument about money exchange had not been settled. One morning we had the question out. Poldek had ambushed me in the hotel lobby, on my surreptitious way to the state cashier's window to change money.

"Thomas, what are you doing?" he asked me with basso incredulity.

"I want to get a bottle of vodka, from the store there."

In the major hotels were stores where, to the chagrin of the Polish populace, tourists and Poles of status in the regime could buy luxury items, including the best of Polish vodka, Wyborowa and Pieprzówka, brands which were normally exported to the USSR.

"Look, I'm just doing it for the experience of it," I told him, though he knew by now that I was a much heartier drinker than most Jews were, and would find a robust vodka comforting in the evenings.

"Give me your money!" growled Leopold. "I'll change it for

you, three times the rate! Why do you go to these crazy little money shops? What is it you have there? A hundred dollars?"

"Poldek," I told him, "I don't like this. You're a grandfather, for God's sake. How about you let me do it legally?"

"*Legal?* Tell me what is legal. What the Russian sons-of-bitch want? Give it to me. I know how it works here."

"How will it work at the airport, when I get arrested?"

"Thomas, dear friend, why do you always worry ahead? Do you think I will let you get in trouble? You? My brother?"

"Even you can't stop it. I'm going to change this legally."

He turned lugubrious. "And so you give in to Jaruzelski? So you don't trust me."

"Don't try that. Of course I trust you."

"Then give me the money."

And so the dispute went. It was a sense that our debate was becoming public, and attracting the attention both of the reception desk staff and the state's cashier behind his grille, that caused me to slip the notes to him.

"Let me come with you," I urged.

"Don't be stupid," Poldek told me.

"You're not a young man, Poldek. I insist."

"I like you like a brother, Thomas, but you haven't lived through things. You volunteer too much information and you talk too loud. You wouldn't have lasted two weeks with the Nazis. They loved killing guys like you. Poetic guys."

"What if your black-market man is a policeman in plain clothes?" I whispered. "An agent provocateur?"

"And you think I couldn't tell the difference?"

Poldek, law-abiding Eagle Scout master of Beverly Hills, saw no reason to respect the laws of Poland as they stood in the late winter of 1981. Soon he was back with the promised zloty, and I bought my bottle of Wyborowa from a lean shopwoman whose weary eyes indicated she might benefit from some luxury items herself.

When Poldek proposed a side trip to Lodz, an industrial city to the west of Warsaw, he had a frank purpose: to visit the graves of Misia's grandparents and her father, the good physician. Misia's mother, Dr. Maria Lewinson, had an unknown, unmarked grave somewhere in the East. Misia's grandparents and father had been worldly successes and assimilating Jews, and they had reached their honored graves in the late 1930s at the end of a normal life span, before the cataclysm. It was because Misia's parents had heard the stories of members of the Camp of National Unity, who resisted the entry of Jews into universities by slashing the faces of pretty Jewish undergraduates, that they had sent her to more subtly anti-Semitic Vienna to study. In addition, Polish universities had a *numerus clausus* (a closed number) for Jewish students, which would have made it difficult for Misia to study in her home country.

I knew that a brief journey to Lodz would be good background, since many of the people who turned up in the Kraków ghetto came from Lodz's quarter of a million Jews. Lodz was fascinating to me also because of all I had read of a remarkable figure named Mordechai Haim Rumkowski, the *Ältester* (Elder) of the *Judenrat*, the Jewish Council in the Lodz ghetto which liaised with the Nazi rulers. Rumkowski had believed

that the ghetto could become a semi-sovereign place where
the Jews could live fruitfully for the duration by making themselves useful to the Nazi regime in Governor-General Frank's
occupied zone. It was a false hope that many of the *Judenräte*
held at the start of the ghetto phase of the Nazi process. On
the basis of that dream, Rumkowski utterly misunderstood his
status and grotesquely entitled himself His Royal Highness,
Prince Rumkowski of Litzmannstadt Ghetto—*Litzmannstadt*
being the German name for Lodz. He produced his own ghetto
currency, with his image on the notes, and ghetto postage
stamps for his postal service, which he named the *Juden-
post*. No doubt he was a vain man, this king of the Jews within
the Lodz ghetto. But then the Jews of Europe had never met
such obliterating intentions as they did in the case of the SS,
and thought that, as in the past, they could bargain their way
out—sacrificing some casualties, perhaps, but allowing a
strong Jewish remnant to survive.

Rumkowski ended up exhorting his populace in the summer of 1944: "Jews of the ghetto, come to your senses! Volunteer for the transports!" When the ghetto was liberated in
January 1945, fewer than nine hundred Jews were found alive.
Rumkowski himself had by then been forced onto a transport
and vanished.

Marek drove us. It was meant to be spring, but if most of the
snow had gone the vividness of spring had not yet arrived. The
forest looked cold, the farms hunched and secretive. Somewhere in the seeping trees near Lodz, Poldek told Marek to
stop and rest, and took me to a sedate but decaying prewar

cemetery graced by its own necropolis railway station where grass grew between the lines and on the platform.

The redheaded cemetery caretaker emerged from his ramshackle residence in that abandoned station house at the cemetery gate. He had the shaggy look of a hunter. Poldek told me that he always left this man some money for the upkeep of Misia's father's and grandparents' graves. The sole visitors, we walked the leaf-muted avenues of the old cemetery, reading the Polish and Hebrew names, admiring splendid monuments and crypts. Poldek found the burial places of Misia's father and her grandparents, muttered that the caretaker had done a passable job of maintenance, and kept a mourning silence with me. Then he coughed.

"Do your Catholic thing," he told me.

"What Catholic thing?"

"Make your cross sign, Thomas. They won't mind."

Though he had overestimated my devoutness, I didn't see why not, so I did it. My tribalism met his. Then, returning to the caretaker's house, Poldek paid him in American dollars for another year's care.

We visited the gray streets of the old ghetto, and then Marek turned our car southeast to Kraków. A thin sun dared fall on the farmlands, which suddenly looked pleasant, timeless and enduring. On the road toward Częstochowa, Marek began to pull up behind, and then pass, truckloads of Russian conscripts. They looked bored and blank, unmarked and extremely young as they stared at us over the tailgates of their vehicles. We were still passing them when we skirted the dark pinnacle of the church-fortress shrine of Częstochowa's miraculous Black Virgin. It struck me that this holy place was sinisterly close to Auschwitz, where other Jewish women had not been venerated at all. But again Poldek seemed awed by the Black Virgin's potent cult, and kept a reverent silence as Marek blessed himself and touched the rosary beads and scapular which hung from his mirror. Poldek told me, "The Polish pope has a great devotion to the Black Virgin."

From here on, I began to feel Poldek's palpable excitement as we approached Kraków from the west. Even the thought that his mother and father had been murdered at relatively nearby Tarnów in an early experiment with carbon monoxide, and his sister in some other death camp, did not seem to restrain the homecoming. The dead had been, in his mind, vindicated by history, and he knew that was all that could happen on earth.

We were staying at Eastern Europe's only Holiday Inn, whose manager was an excellent friend of Poldek's and another of his parcel receivers. I was a little disappointed we weren't staying at the Europa, a hotel right on the market square in the town center, or at the Cracovia. Both were decayed grand hotels much patronized in their heyday by Oskar. The Holiday Inn was, however, only a short distance from all we wanted to visit, and more architecturally pleasant than the name might imply. The young manager was summoned to the door immediately for our arrival, and the manager's respect, combined with the Orbis badge, greased our entry into the hotel. Given our room keys, we said good-bye to wiry little Marek, the friend of Wałęsa, with fraternal best wishes and embraces. For our further adventures, we intended to hire a Fiat—in its various models the most common car seen on the streets of Polish towns.

After we had exchanged heavy hugs with the worthy Marek, and were preparing to go to our rooms, Poldek gave me a solemn warning. If beautiful Polish women came to my door offering themselves in the middle of the night, I was not to accept, since they were certainly agents provocateurs.

Seven

Kraków, not heavily bombed, taken without damage by the Germans in 1939 and similarly overrun by the Russians in 1945, had been left largely intact by the war, and as we stepped out for a walk that night, Poldek uttered his hymns to this city as if ghosts did not inhabit it. He pointed out the ancient cloth hall, the marvelously ornate Sukiennice, and St. Mary's Church in the town square, the Rynek Główny, with a citizen's enthusiasm. Indeed, everything looked gracious here, and built for a happier and more elegant life than history had provided.

Kraków was a city of churches, Romanesque and Gothic, and they were all full of people even in the middle of the day. But it also possessed ancient synagogues, some dating back to the fifteenth century, which in 1981 were abandoned and largely going to ruin. The old residential streets around the square mimicked in some cases the Rococo of Vienna and then the solid Austro-Hungarian style of the eighteenth and early nineteenth centuries. Even so, because of air pollution damage to its stones, the city lacked the film-set atmospherics of old Prague, and Poldek told me it had deteriorated since the period of Nazi occupation when the paradoxical Schindler lived in a good apartment in Straszewskiego Street. After the war the great Stalinist steelworks and planned city of Nowa Huta to the east meant that the gargoyles of St. Mary's, the groins of the stone cloth hall, and the buttresses of the cathedral on Wawel Hill were (and still are today) gritty, their surfaces smudged and eroded by acid rain. Poldek believed it was a deliberate Kremlin policy, to attack the ancient pride of fashionable Kraków with poisonous Stalinist grime. The Rynek Główny, despite the grime, looked to me vast and beautiful and ancient, all of which it was—"Kraków's drawing room," people called it. But of course, Stalin delighted in turning such bourgeois pretensions on their head.

Poldek, as if trying to reconcile me with the Church, graciously insisted on my visiting all the churches with him, and was solemn and prayerful in both splendidly lofty chancel and in minuscule chapel. I was aware that many of his fellow survivors would see the Mariacki, St. Mary's Church, not as a glory of medieval and Renaissance art, but as perhaps yet another pulpit from which for centuries the Jews had been denounced as Christ killers.

After the churches, and after looking at the artworks and linens for sale in the Sukiennice, we walked south to the Vistula and stared up at the castle atop a hill on the riverbank. We began to climb. This was the Wawel, home to Polish dynasties, and here Hitler's darling, former Reich minister without port-folio, SS Obergruppenführer (Lieutenant General) Hans Frank, governed the occupied Government General of Poland territories, the more southerly sector of Poland with Kraków as its capital, for nearly the entirety of the war. It was under him that the major experiments in colonization and resettle-ment of German populations took place, and under him that "the Jewish problem" was addressed most directly. Under Frank, too, the Polish intelligentsia and resistance were slaughtered to the tune of three million, as well as nearly the totality of Poland's Jews. Yet again, the survivor Leopold Pfef-ferberg took me on the first day, and many times after, to the Wawel, and expatiated on its obvious glories, especially its cathedral.

An immense keep faced the ornate cathedral, the church of Poldek's "Polish Pope" (*Polish Pop*) when he was Cardinal-Archbishop of Kraków. The keep and its apartments were more melodramatic and expressive of power than any film lo-cation spotter or artistic director could possibly need. The Wawel was said in prehistory to be the lair of a dragon—his cave can be seen in the hill below. With Frank, of course, the demon emerged at last. It was very easy to imagine the glisten-ing black of Frank's limo-of-state rolling over these cobble-stones toward the stateroom end of the castle square. He made a name for himself even after the war, while in prison, for con-verting to Catholicism and declaring, a penitent all too late, "A thousand years will pass and the guilt of Germany will not be erased."

But again, Poldek seemed to see the place as a site of re-
trieved Polish glory. "The Wawel was Polish a thousand years
ago," he said, "and it's Polish again now." We went into the
cathedral to visit the tomb of St. Stanislav, patron saint of the
nation, and then the Gothic sarcophagus of King Vladislav
Jagiello, founder of the Jagiellonian University. I sometimes
wondered whether, if Poldek stopped viewing these wonders
so positively, he would be destroyed by their significance for
his vanished family and himself.

We strolled from the Wawel to Straszewskiego Street, where
Schindler lived at Number 7, a building a little exorbitantly
decorated in a nineteenth-century sort of way, but in a good
part of town. His apartment had been confiscated from a
middle-class Jewish family named the Nussbaums, who would
end up on Schindler's list. Straszewskiego ran, park to one
side, stylish nineteenth-century buildings on the other, directly from the Wawel.

Before the war, the Pfefferberg family had lived in a similarly comfortable but older Austro-Hungarian-style apartment
building at 48 Grodzka Street, on the other, eastern side of the
Rynek. Standing outside the building—painted cream, which
suited its architecture—Poldek was now overcome by memories of his father, of his mother the interior designer, and of
his young sister, all of them annulled from Europe's history.

From the end of the Napoleonic Wars, when the Congress of
Vienna created a small and sovereign republic of Kraków, a
free city somewhat like Danzig before World War II, Jews who
were considered to have assimilated were permitted to live in

Gentile streets such as this end of Grodzka. Under the Austrians, Poldek Pfefferberg's forebears continued to live in the fashionable parts of Kraków, a little way from the old Jewish ghetto of Kazimierz. Poldek's cream apartment building, of a design one would see in Prague or Vienna itself, stood as a symbol of the tension Jews faced during European history—between secular assimilation and Orthodox memory. This might have been no more the central question of German and Polish Jewry than in the late nineteenth century. The Jews who assimilated into the professions and into Gentile areas hoped that by professional competence and civic loyalty, combined with restrained observance of their religion, they could show themselves to be good citizens of Europe, and so defeat abiding anti-Semitism. Jewish people of the Pfefferbergs' background believed they were enhancing, not diminishing, their Jewishness by the way they lived within the broader culture. Hence Poldek, with a now chastened joy and many understandable references to "son-of-bitch Hans Frank" and other remembered Nazis, stood before the family house where his mother had run her interior decorating office. It was clear now that Poldek saw it unequivocally as home, and also realized that he had been separated from it by treachery. Here, on the run from his guards at Kraków's Glowny station, Poldek first met Oskar, when Herr Schindler came to consult Mrs. Pfefferberg on the interior design of his apartment.

On the street in 1981, as men in their Polish caps passed and looked at us obliquely from under their eyebrows with their perpetual, soul-draining caution, Poldek told me a story which showed how the expropriation of Jewish possessions, the icons of home, still resonated in his dreams. When his mother, father, sister and he had been expelled from this apartment in December 1939 to move to the ghetto, they were forced to leave behind all the furniture. Among the most prized family pieces was a silver lazy Susan, a centerpiece of the Pfefferberg table, ornately wrought by silversmiths and inherited from nineteenth-century grandparents. It would be a small item in the vast SS confiscations, yet infused with the spirit of a family. It was the object, said Poldek, he always looked for in the flea markets of Paris, in the antique shops of London and Prague and New York. He still believed his eyes would alight upon it one day and retrieve it as a memento of his sister, restoring possession to a girl who, caught with her husband living on Aryan papers in Warsaw and shot in Pawiak Prison, had been denied all possessions in death.

Pfefferberg's parents had not been markedly Orthodox Jews but, though they lived in fashionable Grodzka Street, were only a short walk from where Jewish Kraków began, an older and more benign ghetto than the Podgórze ghetto the Nazis set up. This old Jewish quarter of Kazimierz, named to honor King Kazimierz the Great in 1335, was in the old days separated from Kraków by a stream of the Vistula, but since then the growing city had expanded to include it. When we visited, it was a wistful quarter, with only its ancient synagogues to proclaim its vanished Jewishness. Poldek and I walked up Szeroka Street, mounted the steps of the deserted and locked-up Old Synagogue, Stara Bożnica, of the late fourteenth century. Silence ached in its vestibule and in the square it sat on. It was a fascinating building, with a Romanesque look to it, and though it was a tourist site by the time I wrote this sentence, it was certainly not in dour, cramped, hungry 1981. For Poldek it evoked childhood, given his parents had brought him here for Yom Kippur, jollying along their vocal, muscular, fasting son.

It had its strong connection with Schindler, too. Itzhak Stern, the accountant, would later say that Schindler had given him prior warning of the first SS outrage in Kazimierz. An SS party from an *Einsatzgruppe*—an elite "Special Duty Squad"— and policemen of the SD, the *Sicherheitsdienst* or security police, who were also the Party's intelligence wing, moved in to lead the first large raid on the old Jewish ghetto in December 1939. Jewish apartments were plundered, but since this was the first raid of all, people thought that they had the right of protest against such confiscations. It was the hour of prayer at the Old Synagogue, and a number of Jewish householders and families who were not engaged in the prayers in the synagogue were driven there. All were shot, and then the synagogue was set fire to, but was not burned down.

Further up the market square, still in Szeroka Street, Poldek led me to the sixteenth-century Remuh Synagogue. This synagogue was also deserted except for the supervision of one aged Orthodox Jew. In the shaded cemetery, the headstones of Jews from 1551 to about 1800 are crowded in, inscribed with Hebrew. Lining the pathways and shrubbery were cracked gravestones shot up by the Nazis that evening in December 1939, or recovered from the old Jerozolimska Synagogue in Płaszów.

The gravestone fragments from Jerozolimska had been used with both symbolic and engineering intent by the SS to pave the road which led into Płaszów concentration camp. Brought back here after the war, the fragments which could not be fitted together made a wall for a circular wooded shrubbery. Similar pieces leaned round the inside of the high walls of the little cemetery, which had the air of a place unvisited, of deaths forgotten, of gravestones unread.

Kraków. This wonderful city had been Schindler's World War II oyster. He did not go to the market square, however, for its beautiful 700-year-old cloth hall, but to visit the hotels and bars, as well as jazz cellars operating despite official Nazi condemnation of the genre as decadent and Negroid.

Many of Schindler's German peers in Kraków, including Ingrid, whom I had interviewed on Long Island, were *Treuhänder*, German managers put in place to run confiscated Jewish businesses. Schindler, however, always boasted to survivors, and stated in a document written in the late 1950s, that he had taken over a bankrupt enamel business named Rekord, choosing not to be restricted by managing a business as a *Treuhänder* under the regulatory and corrupt German Trust Agency.

I have wondered since, more than I did when writing the book, if *all* the money Schindler gathered to acquire and crank up the business came secretly from Jewish parties whose cash was officially frozen. We know from a number of testimonies that at least a good deal of it did come from these sources. But some might also have come from the Abwehr, German military intelligence.

According to an excellent documentary directed by the Englishman John Blair, sparked by the book and appearing after it, as an Abwehr agent Oskar had played a large part in providing a pretext for the Germans to invade Poland. Blair had managed to find Majola, Goeth's mistress, something Poldek and I did not accomplish. She was dying of emphysema at the time Blair made his documentary, 1983, and comes across on screen as a piteous figure, gasping before the camera. "We were all good Nazis," she wheezed, so close to death that she was not afraid to state these things. "Oskar was a good Nazi." She claimed that in the weeks before the outbreak of war, a memo was sent around to all Abwehr offices asking whether it was possible for anyone to acquire Polish army uniforms. There were no specifics, of course, about the reason for which they were needed, but Schindler—who as a tractor sales rep traveled over the border into Poland all the time, and was based anyhow right on the border at the Abwehr office in Ostrava in Sudetenland—undertook to acquire some. These, claimed Majola, rightly or wrongly, were the Polish uniforms German soldiers wore when they attacked an ethnic German radio station just over the German-Polish border and killed its *volksdeutsch*—ethnic German—staff. These murders were used by Dr. Goebbels and Hitler to justify the German army's advance into Poland to protect their fellow Germans.

If Majola was right, then Schindler had a lot of credit with the Abwehr, and his industrial career would have been partly underwritten by them. Indeed, his Abwehr handlers, Lieutenant Eberhard Gebauer and Lieutenant Martin Plathe, were often in Schindler's company, and he considered them very decent fellows, as indeed they seem to have been. Now Oskar, as an agent-cum-businessman in Kraków, passed on to the Abwehr's Breslau office reports on the plans and behavior of their rivals in the SS, including what he knew about the development of extermination programs. Oskar's Kraków was a complicated place, but he relished it.

Oskar's camp, the Jewish ghetto site and Płaszów were beyond the Vistula and to the south. Poldek and I made our way by tram down Lwowska Street, which had once bisected the Jewish ghetto. Getting off, we walked by way of a few dismal, semi-industrial streets very unlike the glory of the Stare Miasto area near the town square. So we came to undistinguished 4 Lipowa Street, where Schindler had had his office, works and, ultimately, the barracks of DEF, Deutsche Email Fabrik, German Enamel Company, commonly called Emalia by the Jews of Kraków. I recognized the building at once from a photograph Poldek had acquired and shown me—one of Oskar and his office staff standing in front of the entryway of DEF. Oskar stands in the middle of the group, nearly side-on. One can see the front office windows upstairs, from which DEF was run. The staff ranged around him includes Victoria Klonowska, his Polish secretary and red-haired beauty of his front office, with whom he conducted a close relationship simultaneously with his association with Ingrid. Some of his Jewish accountants are there too. A Nazi flag swings from either side of the factory's roofed gateway behind him. Above the entryway, adequate to admit and send forth truckloads of enamelware, someone has painted *4 JAHRE D.E.F.* (Four Years of DEF). This impressive and well-grouped picture was taken in the spring of 1944, the last spring of Emalia, and ultimately Spielberg decided to restage it, as he would restage others of Oskar's and Titsch's photographs, in the ultimate, undreamt-of except by Poldek, film.

In the picture, we can sense behind the faces in this entryway, behind Oskar's huge frame, the presence and industry of the Emalia slave laborers working within, occupying the barracks which Oskar had by now set up behind the factory to save his workers from the risks of being marched back and forth from Commandant Goeth's notorious Płaszów, out in the countryside four miles south.

In gritty Lipowa Street, Poldek and I took in the facade of the building—it was, as Oskar himself said, influenced by the style of Walter Gropius, with large windows fronting the street. Now it was a telephone components factory. The only really vociferous man in Poland, Poldek, entered the building with me and argued at length with a doorman on the lower ground floor, at the base of the stairs which led to what had once been Oskar's office. These stairs Schindler had ascended and descended on business. So had Itzhak Stern, Oskar's accountant, and Abraham Bankier, who was related to the family connected with the bankrupt factory Schindler had acquired. These characters were becoming mythic to me, and yet familiar, and their former occupancy gave the banal building a legendary status.

Poldek at last concluded his argument with the doorman, who picked up the phone and called upstairs. It was in this exact place that, in reality and in the film, Miss Regina Perlman, a good-looking Jewish girl trying to survive on faked Aryan papers, had come to beg Schindler for her parents to be rescued from Płaszów and brought to DEF.

Poldek demanded to speak to the management. An official descended from the upper floor, and Poldek introduced himself and me. The man spoke English with an American accent. We could not possibly be admitted into the manufacturing plant, he said, for among other things the factory was turning out components for the Polish and Soviet army. Poldek now argued with a flattering note of subservience and respect in his voice. He told the man that we were engaged in research into the factory's use in World War II, and could we please just see the main office? At last he consented. We followed him upstairs to a large waiting room where shoddy-looking conductors and pieces of cable were on display, the nonsecret portion of the company's manufacturing. High windows looked down onto the factory floor, where workers did not seem to be imbued with any sense of urgency to turn out the materials needed by the Warsaw Pact armies. The lack of spirit, the dearth of energy which arose from poor diet and crimping of the soul, pervaded the place, and Poldek told me that the Emalia people willingly worked much harder.

In this office, Oskar had, like the true male chauvinist he

was, selected only the most lustrous of Polish secretaries. Ever expansive, he had provided them with Christmas and Easter hams and other black-market luxuries, so that even in the picture taken in 1944, at the height of Polish want, they looked healthy. And to this office, too, Itzhak Stern brought the names of old men, maidens and children who needed particular rescue from Płaszów.

Having grown fraternal with our escort, Poldek now began making extravagant promises to all the officials in this upstairs office. There would be an extraordinary book on Polish wartime heroism! There would also be a film. Please, could he have a card from each of the senior staff? I had already noticed this propensity for card collecting, as if each name Poldek gathered gave him some increment of Polish authority.

At my request we revisited Lipowa Street a number of times during our period in Kraków. Among the avenues of grim industrial Polish architecture, it retained the individuality of its cream color and its covered entryway, but otherwise had no distinction unless the passerby happened to know of its peculiar history.

A relatively short walk eastward, we came to the suburb of Podgórze, site of the wartime Jewish ghetto, which had been set up by a decree of March 3, 1941. People were to enter it by March 20, and any Jew who did not could expect the worst. The Jews of Kraków and a number of other towns, including Tarnów and Lodz, had been crammed in progressively, a family or two or three or five per room, in an area approximately six blocks by four. Walls were erected along Lwowska Street so that trams could pass through without anyone seeing inside the ghetto. The walls of the ghetto were decorated with Middle Eastern–style scallops, rather Egyptian in appearance, to go with the Middle Eastern–style gate of the region the SS would call *Judenstadt*, Jewish Town. Even now, so long after the ghetto had been "liquidated," some of these screening walls were still in place along Lwowska Street.

As in Lodz, the allocation of lodging was under the administration of the *Judenrat*, the Jewish Council, which attempted to allay the situation by cooperating with the authorities, especially now that they believed the very worst, the confiscation of homes and businesses, had occurred. And again, as in Lodz, the Nazis' demands that the *Judenrat* select people for transportation out of the ghetto were met, the *Judenrat* at first sacrificing a few for the many, and then acquiring greater and greater desperate knowledge that the system was a Moloch which wanted the lot. During successive deportations, the people to be transported *Ost*, to the East, were guarded on their way into the trucks by the Jewish ghetto police, the *Ordnungsdienst* (OD), who themselves made a journey from innocence to collaboration, and who liked to believe that their own turn for a journey to oblivion could be averted.

On the day Poldek led me along Jósefinska Street in 1981, the former ghetto was populated chiefly by Catholic Poles. But it didn't seem a place of any great civic joy. The Polish residents knew everything there was to know about the fatuity and dangers of history. Through the street-level entryways one could see courtyards in which muffled children breathed con-

densation into the air and played on wintry ground with antique tricycles as their mothers hung droopy washing. Poldek
showed me the place at 2 Jósefinska Street where he and Misia
had lived as a ghetto-bound young married couple. Here, too,
was the timber yard where during the final ghetto liquidation
in early 1943 he had hidden briefly from the SS, until he heard
the bloodhounds on their way and emerged from hiding just in
time to see the SS and their dogs round the corner toward him.

He took me to a backyard in Limanowskiego Street where in
a cellar during the ghetto days an old man had manufactured
wine for seders and for general consumption, and who had
been raided by the SS and the Polish Green Police and shot
dead. Poldek was expatiating on the tragedy in his normal
basso volume when, looking up, we saw people staring timidly
down at us from gaps between their curtains. "They think
we're KGB or something," Poldek told me. "We're too well
dressed." But one of those who were drawing drapes across
their windows he now recognized. He began shouting to her in
Polish. "Regina darling! *Dzień dobry. Przepraszam!*" He turned
to me. "It is a beautiful girl I knew when I was a boy," he told
me. "I went to the gymnasium with her."

And so we entered a stairwell with its redolence of piss, and
ascended the steps at an earnest pace set by Poldek. We arrived
at the head of the stairs, Poldek calling, "Regina, it's me.
Poldiu Pfefferberg." And at last a door opened a slit. "Remember Poldek Pfefferberg, my dear friend? I became Professor
Magister Leopold Pfefferberg at the gymnasium. But first we
were kids together." The door opened fully. We entered the

room and Poldek looked fondly at the white-haired Polish woman who stood in the hallway, her demeanor marked by nervousness and dignity in equal measure. She stepped back to let us enter, and when we were inside, an older man wearing a yarmulke edged forward from the shadows of the apartment and closed the door behind us. We moved from the corridor into the drawing room. In happier times the apartment had been well designed to admit the sun in winter, but everything was curtained now. No one seemed to want to make eye contact with the treacherous sunlight. The lowered voices of Regina and the old man, and her restrained but friendly reception of Poldek, caused my traveling companion to lower his own voice to the level of what is sometimes called an Irish whisper.

The old man turned out to be not Regina's husband but a fellow Jewish survivor. Regina and the old man were, indeed, two of Kraków's two hundred remaining Jews. Governor General Frank, who had wanted Kraków *judenrein*—clean of Jews— had just about managed it.

Regina switched the lights on in the dim room and it became apparent that this was a little museum. On tables around the edge of the room were ancient-looking kiddush cups, Shabbat candlesticks and trays. There were various silver implements with whose uses I was vaguely familiar—a dented Torah crown, a Havdalah tower. There were occasional parchment fragments of Torah scrolls and, in one case, a scroll in its entirety revealing an illuminated, anciently wrought text. There were fragments from the Torah ark as well, and those silver wands, *yad*s, with a tiny hand at the end of them with which the rabbi traced the holy text.

These artifacts have, by the time I'm writing this, probably been returned to the museum in the Old Synagogue of Kazimierz, a museum which did not exist in 1981. They were remnants from the Old Synagogue of 1570, the little seventeenth-century Remuh Synagogue, beside the extraordinary Remuh cemetery, and the Popov Synagogue, a later building—the three synagogues, that is, of the old Jewish sector named Kazimierz.

Regina insisted now on making all of us *herbata* (tea), and laying out sugar and honey. A few days before, in Kraków, I had visited a state grocery store in which the only items for sale were pickles, soap and mineral water. When a stock of jam or sugar or tea came in, Regina told Poldek, she depended on the grapevine to tell her. Once you got there, you queued for hours. Nor were there any uncomplicated exchanges. Every item required a docket, the docket system being in theory a precaution against the black market. The old man in the yarmulke nodded in confirmation. Survival itself was a test.

At last we left the apartment, Regina at the door trying to hush Poldek's protestations of his abiding admiration of her beauty, and proudly trying to refuse the wad of dollars he passed to her for the museum's upkeep and her own welfare.

Eight

In Poldek's picture collection was a photograph of Oskar, in appropriate equestrian garb, ready to mount a horse for an excursion through the parklands of Kraków. Oskar had told people after the war that in June 1942 he and Ingrid, out riding in a small hilly park named Bednarskiego, south of the ghetto, witnessed one of the first and fiercest *Aktionen*, raids to round up ghetto Jews, children, the aged, and those without the labor documents, the *Blauschein* and *Kennkarte*, and take them away. (That was the day little Genia, a member of the Dresner family, was fruitlessly abroad in her brave red coat.)

Oskar implied that he had had prior knowledge of this *Aktion*, and that he had deliberately placed himself on Bednarskiego. Though the claim that he could have witnessed the *Aktion* from there has been disputed by a subsequent historian, when Poldek took me up among the bare trees in 1981, I found that by walking along it on foot one did have a view of the north/south-running streets of the ghetto (though not of its cross-streets), and I could well imagine the chaos and savagery visible to Oskar at every crossroads in 1942, when the young men of the SS, mothers' sons perverted by the license which was permitted them, now found mothers trying to hide babies, and took the infants by the ankle and smashed them against walls.

I have never believed that the SS were insane—indeed, Himmler said he was very careful to screen out men with murderous pathologies. To make his sane young men believe in the necessity and merit of murder, he changed the language, calling, for example, the corps consigned to the slaughter of Jews behind the front line *Einsatzgruppen*, Special Duty Squads, a sanctifying title.

"That's what I wanted to pointed out," Poldek said after each stop on the ghetto's stations of tears, and the story of each place rendered his little grammatical solecism irrelevant. Such intimacy of horror prevailed in the ghetto! It had been a cramped neighborhood. Poldek showed me the location of the fever hospital, where patients who could not rise were killed in their beds before the eyes of the medical staff, who were themselves about to die. In the general hospital, in the ghetto's western border near the uniform factory of a kindly Austrian, Julius Madritsch, the doctors and nurses fed a merciful dose of strychnine to the patients, so that the SS found only corpses.

Plac Zgody, Peace Place, was a short walk eastward, past Regina's little museum. It was a backwater in 1981. But here in the ghetto days, as well as at the nearby Optima factory, people selected in the *Aktionen* were forcibly loaded onto trucks. In

Plac Zgody forty or so years before our visit, each act of minor defiance by them caused an addition to the heap of corpses on the pavement.

Some thousands whom Oskar observed being collected for the transport that summer day in 1942 were, he discovered, gassed in carbon monoxide chambers at Belzec camp to the east of Kraków, or in specially designed Renault vehicles. Oskar found out about this extermination, it seems, as part of his work for the Abwehr, who wished to keep an eye on these improbable events. The gassing of people had begun, but its "camouflage name" was, even by early 1943 when the ghetto was finally liquidated, "Special Treatment" (*Sonderbehandlung*). The screening to separate people for extermination from those who could still labor was entitled *Gesundheitsaktion*—"Health Action."

In Plac Zgody, I had heard from all the survivors I had so far interviewed, lay the pharmacy of Tadeusz Pankiewitz. He was a Gentile apothecary permitted to remain in the ghetto, and though increasingly deprived of drugs, he had served the Jews heroically. The pharmacy still stood in the square in 1981, a plaque on its wall to honor the man who would rush forth in the face of armed SS to try to treat those summarily shot in the ghetto's roundups and last hours. Poldek said he had got to know the pharmacist Pankiewitz well, through his own journeys in and out of the ghetto. With his high Slavic cheekbones, Poldek could easily pass as a Gentile Pole and had been a frequent errand runner for the *Judenrat*, the Jewish Council, and for others.

One of Poldek's reasons for moving in and out of the ghetto

by crossing Plac Zgody and passing through the fanciful Arabian gate into Lwowska Street, where trams could be caught to central Kraków, was the creation by the Nazis of a new monetary unit banned to Jews. At considerable personal risk, he would carry the funds of ghetto individuals and organizations to town, where he would exchange them for the new, safer currency at as small a discount as he could negotiate with Gentile money-dealers, who were permitted to use both currencies. No wonder he was not scared of government exchanges and back-lane currency deals! I'd heard this from others—that Poldek was good at these tasks, which he pursued without wearing his Star of David and thus under pain of summary execution.

Poldek spoke with affection of a German policeman he used to meet on the gate, Wachtmeister Oswald Bosko, a devout Catholic in a way Oskar wasn't, who would let food and medicines be smuggled into the ghetto without the necessity of a bribe. At a stage when people didn't know whether their children were safer within the walls or out of them, Bosko let children be smuggled in and out, since they would face being shipped off or shot if they entered or left openly. Ryszard Horowitz, future renowned photographer, was smuggled in from a hiding place outside to join his parents, whom he was missing; his playmate Roman Polanski was smuggled out. Oswald Bosko would ultimately be arrested for his pro-Jewish activities, tried and executed. He has been honored by Yad Vashem in Jerusalem, yet poignantly there is no extant photograph of this decent soul.

We had nearly finished trawling the ghetto, drawing at every turn suspicious looks as Poldek dragged me into courtyards and along piss-streaked pavements. He pointed out such features as the old Polish Savings Bank, where people came to get the certificates they needed for their survival. He had not been issued a *Blauschein* once, and had nearly been sent off in a truck, purely because his then occupation, tutoring the children of Symche Spira, the self-important head of the ghetto police, was not considered essential.

If a prisoner survived the ghetto and its liquidation by the SS officer Amon Goeth, the next stage of the process was detention in the new camp of Płaszów. Płaszów was at the time in Kraków's rural fringe, four miles southeast of the city on the road to Lwów. By 1981 it was still a huge, open acreage, though partially impinged upon by new houses. What the prisoners always called the commandant's "villa" still stood, surrounded by the villas of his senior officers. On the drizzly spring day Poldek and I walked past them, they were occupied, of course, by Polish tenants again. In their ordinary stucco—in Hannah Arendt's much publicized phrase—"the banality of evil" was still evident.

The core of what had been the camp was a vast field with, at one end, the encroaching city, and at the other the notorious old Austro-Hungarian hill fort which had once guarded the road to Lwów, a mounded enclosure nicknamed by locals Chujowa Górka, Prick Hill. In this screened-off place the executions of thousands of Poles and Jews were carried out. Slaughtered or buried in it were Jews found living under Aryan papers; members of the Jewish resistance, the ZOB, who had blown up a Wehrmacht and SS café, the Cyganeria in Kraków; Polish partisans, both Gentile and Jew; and those summarily executed by gunshot or hanging within the camp, such as Lisiek, Goeth's house and stable boy, who was shot dead for supposedly mishandling Goeth's saddle. When the Russians got close, sooner than the SS had calculated they would, many able-bodied guards and prisoners were employed to dig up the graves and burn the remains on pyres, a scene which, as the dead sat up and even seemed to dance in the flames, sent some people, including an SS NCO, temporarily insane. Poldek had been there, working like crazy to avoid a bullet, seeing the bodies gesticulate in the flames as he breathed through his rag mask and wept.

Nearby, on a low rise, stands a postwar monument of four giant sculpted figures, riven pieces of stone in stylized human form, to commemorate the victims. In these green fields enough agony occurred to make Płaszów a byword for cruelty, if it had not been for the fact that the SS had also devised and implemented the ultimate, the destruction camp, of which Auschwitz was the archetype.

Poldek was exceptionally sober and undemonstrative as he showed me where the Ukrainian barracks were; the *Puffhaus*—brothel—for the SS; the women's camp; the men's; the *Appellplatz* or parade ground where random executions also took place during roll call. I took photographs of everything, but they were not necessary. I can still bring to mind the camp plan, the green bed of the fort where the brave and the adventurous died, and the starkness of those part-fractured, soulful pillars of stone, the acid rain of Nowa Huta working a new chemistry upon them. The geography is still engraved on my brain by the force of the events I heard of there. I was astonished by Poldek's capacity to revisit the place, to exercise distance, to be a solemn tourist to his own past misery.

When the SS closed down the Kraków ghetto and sent everyone either to labor camps (*Zwangsarbeitslager*), or to destruction camps (*Vernichtungslager*) for *Sonderbehandlung*, Schindler was given, as those who have read the book might remember, the option of placing DEF inside this new camp at Płaszów. Oskar's fellow entrepreneur, Julius Madritsch, *would* locate his uniform factory inside Płaszów camp. Oskar had rejected the idea, not wanting to be under anyone's close inspection, and that was why each day his workers were marched to Emalia in Lipowa Street, and—until Oskar put in his own barracks—came back under guard in the evening to the barracks of Płaszów.

We met for tea another of the child survivors of the Holocaust, Niusia Horowitz, Ryszard's sister, who still lived in Kraków and was a beautician at the Hotel Europa. Her married name was Karakulska. It did not seem to be an irony to her to be working on the faces of the privileged and of tourists in a hotel which, during her enslavement, had been much patronized by the Nazis. But she was nervous about having to meet this stranger from the Antipodes, under the eccentric aegis of Uncle Poldek, and to have to talk about the ghetto and Amon Goeth's Płaszów, and her weeks in Auschwitz, and the role of Herr Direktor Schindler in her family's deliverance.

We drank tea in one of the many splendid cafés around the Rynek. Insofar as Poles and the remaining hundreds of Polish Jews were able, she had made a life for herself, but again, it was palpable in the delicate fidgeting of her fingers on the *herbata* glass that the children had suffered worst, found recall most painful, and that although she said she wanted to give this interview, she was doing so through gratitude to Oskar, fear of Poldek, and perhaps clan solidarity with her parents and brother. An adult prisoner knew at least that those who were oppressing him were working within their own coherent if misguided picture of the universe. Even if, as in the case of Goeth, that coherent picture sanctioned random shooting of prisoners—a form of rifle practice and of keeping the inmates on their toes—the adult prisoner still knew what Goeth was getting at. The child prisoner was more radically disoriented by such events. They could not be absorbed. They could certainly not be interpreted.

Niusia and Ryszard Horowitz's father, Dolek Horowitz, had been an important purchasing officer inside Płaszów camp, and was allowed to have his children with him. But as other children began to disappear, Niusia, his tall ten-year-old daughter who cut her fingers sewing bristles onto the backs of broomheads in the brush factory, kept seeing trucks arriving at the Austrian hill fort of Chujowa Górka, followed by a racket of guns firing, and was in a terrible mental state. So Dolek pleaded with Stern to get the family moved to Emalia, Oskar's place. Niusia became one of those children who Schindler insisted must be retained in his camp because only their delicate fingers could polish the interior of his smaller-caliber artillery shells.

Poldek also took me to see his old anatomy professor, Dr. Lax, who lived in what Poldek called "an intellectual's apartment from the 1930s." In its way, since Hitler had as many Polish intellectuals shot as he could manage, the apartment was a museum of the period. It was spacious but dominated by somber Polish impressionists, and heavy-bound volumes of Polish and French literature and anatomy. Dr. Lax was tall and frail, a survivor both as a scholar and a Jew, and Poldek spoke to him with a rumble of reverence.

During the war, the secular Lax had seen no reason why young men should be arrested as Jews purely on the grounds of their having been circumcised. But the Gentile majority in Europe were not circumcised, and unless the circumcised male could produce a document proving circumcision on medical grounds, he was considered Jewish. Lax had himself organized a few such certificates but had also devised a method for lengthening the foreskin of secularized Jews who considered themselves Europeans, and thus felt they had every right to go on breathing as much European air as they needed. This method of Dr. Lax's involved an often very painful sequence of foreskin stretching, which would have sounded funny had the life of individual young men not depended upon it. Sometimes tyrants do away with the necessity of satire by imposing absurdity themselves.

Lax had remained dangerously at large during the war, worked as a doctor with the partisans, survived, and had now come to the full honor of his old age. He had been involved not only with the forest partisans but with those who operated in town, terrorists in the eyes of the German authorities, who blew up a German forces cinema and bombed cafés used by the Wehrmacht and SS.

Still the spring sunshine seemed merely condi-tional, as if the earth's default setting would remain rain and mist. The countryside to the west of Kraków still showed rem-nants of snow everywhere, and bare trees seemed under an edict not to bud as we journeyed through them. Oświęcim, the town from whose German-version name, Auschwitz, the camps took their sinister umbrella repute, seemed a normal place, with stores and coffee shops, a community refusing to be tied to or inhibited by its own unfortunate and unchosen associations. Indeed, to be fair, it's hard to know, had they been sure of everything that was happening a few miles from town, *and* been shocked by it, what an ordinary citizen could have done about the camps. One could so easily succumb to that all-too-human denial which is an inherited gift of all members of the species.

Auschwitz 1, the first of the camps, was designed for Rus-sian prisoners and political prisoners, and for medical exper-iments on children, twins and women. Hangings, detention of people in absurdly small spaces, and obscene medical exami-nations were the order of the day in this first camp, close to the villa of the commandant of the entire Auschwitz system,

Rudolf Höss. It is the camp which carries over the gate in wrought iron the renowned improving adage *ARBEIT MACHT FREI*— Work Makes One Free. (It was from a barracks at Auschwitz 1 that the child Ryszard Horowitz, until then surplus to experimental requirements, was liberated at the end of the war.)

Auschwitz 2, also called Auschwitz-Birkenau, was a massive area, death's anteroom for numberless Jews from Ruthenia to Greece to Paris. It was reached via a gate through which the trains arrived full from all over the Reich, and departed empty. This is the camp which above all plays on our imagination, for it was in Auschwitz 2 that, having found through experimentation the correct asphyxiant gas, the Nazis were able to produce death as an industrial outcome, and to attend to the greatest problem, the obliteration of the remains, in industrial ovens. Walking down the lanes of Auschwitz 2, one can feel the *accidie*, the operational ennui which produced the daily results. As in any factory, many of the SS workers were bored with the process and were driven, as happened in the famous scene in the book and movie *Sophie's Choice*, to play games to relieve the monotony in this extraordinary place in which humans were reduced to a whisper from a chimney.

Huge Auschwitz 2 was largely demolished, and the gas chambers and ovens dynamited, as the Russians drew close, but there is enough material remaining to horrify. The railway itself, with its archway, would be used by Spielberg in the film that at this point no one but Poldek dreamed of, and is still capable of carrying a large locomotive and rolling stock. The huts were thin-walled, unlined and inadequate for winter. When one goes to the western end of the camp and descends the stairs into the chambers, it takes an effort to walk to the middle of the space. An irrational fear arises that the door might be closed and, through the nozzles in the roof, a vaporous death enter.

I found it hard to believe that those Schindler women I had met, those faces of familial normality, had been caught here in Auschwitz 2 in 1944 as potential oven fodder. As I would write, there were a number of versions of the story of how the Schindler women had survived the place and then been shipped out to Brinnlitz. Their rescue is universally attributed by former prisoners to Schindler. A number of male prisoners claim independently of each other to have approached Oskar when their womenfolk did not arrive in Brinnlitz. Some say he paid diamonds, others that he sent one of his better-looking secretaries to talk to and if necessary give herself to officials. That the women survived is assured. That Misia Pfefferberg and Leosia Korn, Manci Rosner and Niusia Horowitz, were rescued is a matter of fact.

We had a little time now to drive to the mountains and look over the Danube toward Oskar's hometown, Svitavy—Zwittau— and the site of his long-vanished Brinnlitz camp. We decided we would need to come back later in the year, but the truth is that we never did. The writing of the book would begin under pressure of ingested tales, and claim all the coming months.

One morning in Kraków between two and three I was awakened by a knocking at the door of my room. I thought it might have been restless Poldek, with more information to impart.

When I opened up, I found an exquisite and very drunken Polish girl, perhaps twenty-five years old, wrapped only in a blanket and otherwise apparently naked, asking for a light. It is likely she had been working from room to room. She didn't look like an agent provocateur of the kind Poldek had warned me of. She could have modeled for a statue of Polonia, the nation, but a Polonia worked over by tyranny and vicious times. Yeats saw Ireland itself similarly, incarnated in his character Kathleen Ni Houlihan, a woman formerly beautiful but now misused and debauched. Of course, I did not think too deeply along these lines at the time. She was magnificent, whatever her purpose, but all too blatantly a victim. I hope it was virtue which made me send her away. In any case, out of mischief I gave her Poldek's room number and told her he had a light.

This girl somehow became confused in my head with that anthem that was played each noon on Polish radio—one clear, melodic trumpet call originally played, at least according to legend, from the steeple of St. Mary's Church in Kraków, and stopped mid-note at the point that a Tartar arrow struck the trumpeter. This interrupted melody, a combination of unfinished business and violated spirit, was known as the *Hejnał Mariacki*.

```
Nine
```

The night was dank when we went to the airport at Kraków to catch our plane out of the Poland of fears and whispers, and to Vienna. Early in the afternoon I had asked Poldek about dumping some of our plentiful zloty. He had told me, "Don't be a worrier. They won't even ask us—they won't make a fuss when they see my Orbis badge."

But having arrived in the dimly lit terminal we ran into exactly the trouble I had feared, and Poldek's Orbis badge proved, for once, inadequate protection. We were required to change our zloty back into U.S. dollars at the government exchange booth, and when we did so we had more dollars than were accounted for by hotel and food receipts. An official in a blue uniform to whom I presented my papers saw the difference and seemed very disturbed by us. He led us away from passport control, which lay between us and our exit to some happier land, and took us to a desk far off on the flank of the airport terminal, and into an office full of men in greenish paramilitary uniforms, some of them bearing semiautomatic weapons. The official assigned to us was one of the latter. His Kalashnikov strapped very martially to his chest, he began looking at our papers and passports. It has to be remembered that in 1981 such procedures and such publicly displayed arms were not common in the West, and were of their nature more alarming than they would be now. But Poldek seemed un-amazed. He whispered to me to get out my latest novel again, a copy I was taking to Moshe Bejski, Schindler's former forger, now an Israeli Supreme Court justice.

Meanwhile, the official pursed his lips over my financial document and the latest exchange document I had. He began speaking in Polish with a lazy hostility. Poldek answered him loudly, as if trying to smother him in fearlessness. According to him, I was prodigiously well-known, a virtual Hemingway. (Technically that could be said of any novelist—they were all prodigiously well-known by their small readership.) And here we had been in Poland, Poldek asserted, for research for a multimillion-dollar film concerning World War II Polish his-tory. The film would win the Academy Award, Poldek assured the fellow. Everyone, he said, agreed with that. Obviously, he implied, we were so focused on injecting millions of dollars into the Polish economy that we hadn't had much time to sort out small matters concerning zloty.

Now he pulled from his pocket every card he had gathered in every office and from every official we had met, including the young manager of the Holiday Inn in Kraków and the offi-cials of the telephone components company we had met in Os-

kar's old factory. All these gentlemen en masse, he said, were
ecstatic at our efforts, and right behind us, and anxious that no
hindrance be placed in our path. The thought of so many millions of dollars in production money delighted them—and they
were, of course, all significant men and, by gentle implication,
men with the power to make this uniformed fellow miserable.

Poldek did not once tell the man that our heroic Polish book
was not yet written, but he showed him the book he had taken
from me. An American hardcover edition of a novel was indeed a remarkable artifact by the standards of Poland then, its
books being produced with limp, tearable covers on thin,
speckled and yellowing paper. The official thumbed through
its thick-napped pages and checked me against my picture on
the inside back cover. Even so, I was waiting for this monetary
cop or whatever he was to turn on Poldek angrily and tell him
to be silent, and to call in other officers to help deal with us
for exchange crimes. It was now, as the man absorbed and
weighed my book and what had been said, that Poldek went
beyond the bounds of credibility.

"And don't you think, Thomas," he asked, "that this man
has exactly the sort of heroic Slavic features we need for our
film? Sir, sir, if you would be so kind, could we have your name
and address?"

The man's eyes nearly closed and became ambiguous slits. I
was sure the screaming and gun-pointing would begin now.

"Here, I have paper, my friend," Poldek announced, tearing
a page out of a notebook and offering it to the official. The
man's brow unclenched and he broke into a sneer, or so I

thought. It grew, however—and to my astonishment—to become an authentic grin of delight. Suddenly the man was handing back my book and joking in Polish with Poldek. He leaned over our financial statements still on the table but no longer a matter of primary concern, and took up a ballpoint pen. I remember that he seemed to write in urgent hope in sharp-edged Polish script. He wanted to escape the address he was putting down on paper. I could not believe that such egregious and transparent balderdash as Poldek had brought to bear had produced this new geniality at the counter. When the man had finished writing he held the page up like a student offering his essay to a teacher. In this case, to Professor Magister Pfefferberg.

Analyzing all this later, I realized that even had I the daring to offer an inducement anyone should have been able to see through, I would have revived suspicion in the guard behind the counter. But Poldek knew instinctively that when persiflage reaches its apogee, it must be maintained unapologetically and without apparent fear or rush, and its intensity retreated from only gradually. Poldek took out his wallet, kissed the man's name and address before folding the page deftly with his free hand and placing it within the wallet. After he had returned the wallet to his breast pocket, he kissed his fingers, a Polish gesture which implied the data he had just deposited was sacred.

"I shall wear this by my heart," he told the policeman, "until I return to Beverly Hills."

Almost as an afterthought, the man stamped my statement.

Poldek shook his hand enthusiastically and asked him about his children. Then, with undue awe, the man shook my hand too.

I had left what the West considered repressive countries for "liberal" destinations before—Beijing to British Hong Kong, for example. The contrast had not been as starkly revealed, though, as in the short aircraft journey from Poland to Vienna. The center of Vienna seemed exquisite and exuberantly lit in a way that, despite a sinister history, defied all fear and whispers. We stayed at a hotel which had once accommodated Hitler, and I felt the delirium of Vienna's brighter air.

One of our chief objectives now was to trace Goeth's family—they had owned a printing company. There was no printing company of that name in the Vienna business registry or in the phone book. Nor did we yet know that in a nearby apartment Goeth's embittered former mistress Majola was dying of emphysema.

At the Adlon Hotel, within sight of that wonderful cathedral the Stephansdom, we interviewed two survivors, fashionably dressed Viennese, the Hirschfelds; and another survivor who wished to be identified in the book by the letter *M*. M was an interior designer in Vienna, but had witnessed, as a prisoner, the killing of Polish women in the old Austrian fort to the southwest of Płaszów camp, on Chujowa Górka. During these interviews, as ever, I made tape recordings and took notes as well, a frenetic combination, belt and braces, but justified by the honor all these *Schindlerjuden* had done me in granting me interviews, even under the compelling aegis of Poldek. We and the Hirschfelds had a Martell brandy together at the end of the evening, in honor of Oskar's own passion for brandy.

Another Viennese we made contact with was Mrs. Bankier, the widow of Oskar's factory manager, a man who had much honor among his fellow survivors. It was Bankier—not, as the film has it, Itzhak Stern—whom Oskar rescued from a transport to the east one morning at Prokocim Station. He had been found without his *Kennkarte* and his *Blauschein*. He had also been related to the former owners of Rekord, the company Oskar took over.

We failed to find Goeth's relatives, despite the helpful suggestions of the Hirschfelds and Mrs. Bankier. Understandably, they had never tried to seek them out, and only a tiger like Poldek could contemplate meeting them in polite surroundings. I was certainly uneasy about interviewing them, about asking them to fill me in on the childhood and young manhood of Amon. In any case, Vienna was something of a whistle-stop on the way to the cornucopia of *Schindlerjuden* which Israel would offer.

Our dawn landing at Ben Gurion airport in Tel Aviv caused many passengers to sing and others to become meditative. Many stepped to the side of the stairway on descending from the plane and kissed the cool morning tarmac. It was now full spring, and the griefs and terrors of the Israeli-Palestinian conflict seemed far away from Tel Aviv, beyond the Golan Heights. To look upon the string of hotels along the beachfront, one would see Tel Aviv as a pleasure port. But for Arabs as for Jews, it could be a place of ferocious memory.

Israel, at that time an unusually rigorous processor of boarding and disembarking travelers, had nonetheless let through as baggage a strange item, the Zakopanean ice pick Poldek had insisted on buying for me in the Sukiennice in Kraków. To someone not accustomed to the Polish mountains south of Kraków, it was a strange implement: a wooden shaft, highly ornamented, with metal casings from which little rings hung. At one end it sported an ice spike, and at the other an ornamental ax blade. I had consigned it to the baggage hold because I hoped the Austrian or Israeli security would confiscate it. Perhaps the baggage officials who no doubt inspected it were familiar with such things and considered it purely decorative. Yet it was as potentially lethal as a combination baseball bat, gouger and ax. I would in fact be accompanied by it all the way back to Australia, through many airports, ever hoping that someone in their right mind would consider it too perilous to tranship. But always, as I waited for my luggage, its jaunty blade and metallic fixings would jerk up the conveyor belt at the top of the baggage carousel, and I would in the end find I was stuck with the thing for life.

Our arrival in Israel brought the question home to me, the one I always knew I would have to face. I sympathized greatly with the Palestinians. I saw them, simplistically no doubt, as having paid the ultimate price for European anti-Semitism. European culture, through the Nazis and their collaborators, could not have made it clearer to Jews that Europe had never been and would never be a safe place for them. Europe's rivers of anti-Semitism still ran robustly underground in the post–World War II period. I could well understand the political passion of Zionism to find an unassailable nation of one's own, better than I could grasp the religious fervor which also sometimes went into it.

The constitution of another oppressed people, the Irish, demonstrated behind its powerful civic pieties the uneasy relationship between the bureaucracy of the Catholic Church and the liberal democracy which was the true aspiration of the Irish people. The same conundrum faced Israel, and would come to bedevil it more and more. And glib European claims that the Jews and their *Judenräte* sometimes connived at their own destruction by showing passivity (though there wasn't much passivity in the Warsaw Ghetto uprising!) were something the Israelis were bound to react to by becoming militarily ruthless. "Never again!" was the cry. So European malice created not only the original calamity but a determination in the Middle East that never again would Jews be accused of collaborating in their own destruction. The Palestinians bore the brunt of this rigorousness.

I knew that trying to tell a story which, because of its human scale, made it possible for readers to *imagine* the Holocaust, could be seen by some as an encouragement to Israeli hardliners. This was not a trite concern. Naturally, by now, I wanted to attempt the book, especially having heard the tale from so many mouths, and particularly since with its moral puzzles about Oskar's character it exerted a particular attraction. I was aware that some Irish historians believed any dwelling on, or overemphasis of, the catastrophes of Irish history, particularly the Famine, encouraged the Provisional IRA in its explosive campaigns in Northern Ireland and the British mainland. Years later, I would come under a multipaged attack by Fintan O'Toole, Irish revisionist commentator, in *The New Republic*, for my history of the Irish world, *The Great Shame*, from the point of view of Irish political prisoners transported to Australia. The Germans had their own *Historikerstreite*, historical conflicts, about Nazism and the Holocaust, what should be made of them and what should be emphasized and de-emphasized, and what the political consequences might be of history written in a particular style. And in Australia there were many historiographical, and thus political, debates over both the nature of convictism and the legitimacy of Australian settlement in light of the dispossession of the Aboriginals.

But then what is the alternative to trying to tell the truth about the Holocaust, the Famine, the Armenian genocide, the injustice of dispossession in the Americas and Australia? That everyone should be reduced to silence? To pretend that the Holocaust was the work merely of a well-armed minority who didn't do as much harm as is claimed—and likewise, to argue that the Irish Famine was either an inevitability or the fault of the Irish—is to say that both were mere unreliable rumors, and not the great motors of history they so obviously proved to be. It suited me to think so at the time, but still I believe it to be true, that if there are going to be areas of history which are off-bounds, then in principle we are reduced to fudging, to cosmetic narrative. Thus, though worried, I was defiant in my intention to write this book.

Poldek's excitement at being here after our night flight seemed not so much because he was back on an ultimate ancestral land, but because he was about to meet so many of his friends again. He had come here with Oskar and Gosch and the screenwriter Koch nearly twenty years before. But he made sure we stayed in the same beachside hotel in the Marina area as Oskar had then, where the Mediterranean came surging in on an enormous beach full of the muscular and shining young.

After a nap and a bracing shower, and no time for swimming—we were not here for that—Poldek led me out to a marketplace, the little jewelry stall of Helen Hirsch. Hirsch was the handsome woman who, when a young prisoner, had been chosen by Amon Goeth to be his housekeeper. She had suffered many strange and frightening experiences in Goeth's villa, and her hearing in one ear was still permanently impaired from a blow he had given her. Goeth had seemed in part attracted to her, in part repelled. Now she was in late middle age, married, and still making an adequate living out of selling her Middle Eastern style filigreed jewelry. I bought from her two filigreed *hamsehs*, open hands with the eye of God in the palm. In Goeth's kitchen, though, she had not been aware of any particular divine vigilance over her.

She was not exactly a vocal woman, but in a lowered voice

she would tell me a number of tales of Schindler visiting her in the kitchen of the villa at Płaszów where she was Goeth's slave and the butt of his unreliable fury. Schindler had told her toward the end of the camp's existence that he got her on the list for the Brinnlitz camp by winning a hand of vingt-et-un, blackjack, against Goeth. In telling the story, Oskar showed a man-of-action indifference to the question of what would have happened to her had he lost the hand. He simply possessed an ill-advised confidence that he always won at cards. Fortunately for her, she also survived the changes introduced into the list by the corrupt Jewish clerk-cum-policeman Marcel Goldberg.

Since Oskar had such a reputation as a womanizer and charmer, and since the Schindler women understood this, there was always the question of whether his kindness had a sexual motive. Manci Rosner of New York, grandmother, matriarch and survivor—as well as other women survivors—had answered the question in her own way. "You should have seen the women he had. Beautiful women, healthy women, in beautiful dresses. He should want me, covered with lice?" Helen in Tel Aviv said, "Schindler was Schindler. You can't argue about him. He was what he was. His motives you couldn't guess and, being who he was, they made sense only to him. In some ways he was crazy."

From Helen Hirsch, Itzhak Stern's wife Dr. Sophia Stern, and the Dresner and Schindel families, I got a sense of what a haven Oskar found in Israel in the 1960s. Even so, he always returned in the end to his little apartment in Hauptbahnstrasse in Frankfurt. His survivors were middle-class people here—the successful thoracic physician Dr. Idek Schindel, for example, and the Dresners. Dr. Schindel, who gave me some treatment for the congestion I'd developed in Poland, told me he had said to Oskar one night in the 1960s, "Oskar, you are very welcome in my home, but you cannot have more than two brandies." Schindel said Oskar took that restriction with good grace, but left early to go to his hotel bar.

Danka Dresner, who had been a child during the war years, told me of her parents' attempts to shelter her and her brothers from Health Actions and the various combings of the ghetto by SS and Jewish OD personnel, some of whom overlooked Danka because of their previous friendship with the family. Danka Dresner, like Niusia Horowitz, became one of those children who Oskar claimed were essential to his war efforts for polishing the insides of small-caliber shells.

The little girl who wore red, Genia, was the cousin of Danka Dresner, and her guardian in the camp was Dr. Idek Schindel, then a young ghetto doctor and also a cousin of the Dresners. She had previously been hidden by a family outside, but then had wanted to be with her parents in the ghetto. Yet by the time of the clearance of the ghetto, Genia's parents had vanished, and so she became the ward of Idek, who had a lively, whimsical character and was more than capable of entertaining and calming such a child. It was during the first large clearance of the ghetto in 1942—the gleaning out of some seven thousand people, including children—that Genia made her now famous walk. Dr. Schindel was fully occupied at the ghetto hospital, where there were many fever and malnutrition cases, and Genia had hidden herself for a time, as her uncle had advised her to do if ever this sort of thing were to happen. Then, as if drawn by the magnetism of events outside, she emerged and walked the streets, small fry seemingly ignored by the SS, and then returned to her normal or some other hiding place.

Her walk through the ghetto, which Spielberg would honor with one of the few patches of color in the otherwise black-and-white film, was noticed with amazement and concern by some of her relatives, including the preadolescent Danka and her mother. Living on for the time being, Genia survived until the final liquidation of the ghetto the next year, and then vanished. Danka said she had died in Auschwitz. The loneliness of her death, the sense of abandonment which went along with the bullet or the gas, is hard to countenance and bear—though I would later see similar tragedies overtake East African children living in fear and exercising unavailing valor.

The Dresners took to feeding Poldek and myself royally in their house in Tel Aviv, and so did Dr. Idek Schindel, who liked to make jokes about my having "a strongly developed gag response" when he'd examined me. I had not always had that; surely it could not be the regular tales of asphyxiation and sudden death that had made my throat overreactive?

Dr. Sophia Stern, wife of Oskar's late accountant, Itzhak Stern, had passed over to me for copying her husband's documents and speeches relating to Oskar's war record. Among these was a highly useful published tract which Itzhak had written in honor of Julius Madritsch, the Austrian owner of the uniform factory in Płaszów. I had heard Madritsch praised by Misia and others; and in Israel, too, I heard nothing but good of him. If from the point of view of history he had a fault, it was that in 1944, having perceived the full intent of the Nazis, he despaired of the survival of his Jews as any sane man would have. By then he had concluded on good evidence that the destruction machine would get them all. But while there was always ambiguity in Oskar's tale, Madritsch was a more predictably decent fellow. In Itzhak's mind, his virtues—his provision of extra rations for his prisoners; his willingness to protect them from SS brutality while they were inside the factory—needed acknowledgment. For the system had given him plenty of license to be a brute, and he was not. Some other German institutions behaved well too, but some of the largest, most famous corporations did nothing effective to try to ameliorate the inhuman treatment of their slave workers. Stern's limited-edition tract in German, printed on glossy paper to honor its subject, was entitled *Menschen in Not*—Humans in Need.

Poldek was predictably delighted to be reunited with these people, breathing and laughing despite the intentions of the Reich. He amply praised the agelessness of the Dresner women and of Dr. Stern, and I could see he meant it all, since he loved them all, those girls who'd been young when he was young and whose survival shone in them. Like many monogamous men, he liked women, whereas the "liking" extended by Schindler, though it obviously brought fond memories to many women other than his wife, was not as reliable a commodity.

We were rarely at our hotel. We were out continuously, talking about Schindler. In one house a former prisoner said, "Remember all the jokes in Płaszów?" Shut in at night, the subhumans had room for laughter. And then another said, "And remember how much screwing there was! People screwed like crazy in the camp." A defiance of death, I guessed, never having been on the edge of the pit like these people. A defiance of Amon on his balcony with his sniper's rifle.

When not dining at survivors' houses, Poldek and I liked to go to the Romanian restaurant up by Ben Yehuda Street where Oskar was well remembered and where he had always dined free of charge, and lingered over Martell and Metaxa brandies. In the Romanian restaurant, Poldek mentioned to me an elderly fellow named Shmuel or Samuel Springmann who lived in Ramat Gan, a northeastern suburb of the city. Springmann had been one of the founders of the Jewish Relief and Rescue Organization which operated from Istanbul. He had sent his agents into Europe to get information from well-placed people about the situation in Poland and Germany. One of his agents was a Dr. Sedlacek, a dentist, who went to Kraków and made contact with Oskar at the factory in Lipowa Street. As authorized by Springmann's organization, Sedlacek passed on to Oskar money supplied ultimately from New York, for the purchase of fake passports and other documents for various Jews. After the war, Oskar always boasted that he had used Relief and Rescue money impeccably, though he wasn't sure about some of the other people Relief and Rescue used. Some of them were semi-criminal operators, he complained to Sedlacek. He felt very prudish about them, Sedlacek would later report.

Since Oskar was still an agent of the Abwehr, he had plenty
to tell Sedlacek about the destruction camps, which had begun
their work in 1942 with carbon monoxide gassing. Within the
chambers of Belzec, it had taken an hour or more to kill the
scrambling, writhing mass. The SS were trying to find a more
"humane" and faster method. At Sedlacek's urging, Oskar
agreed to go to Budapest, which was then not directly under
Nazi control, and meet with Springmann and others. It was to
find out what happened at that meeting that we wished to visit
the aging Mr. Springmann.

We took a cab out to Ramat Gan and, in a park, met up with
him. He had nominated the park because he said his apartment was not spacious enough to entertain people. Springmann's mind seemed sharp but his general health was in clear
decline. He was accompanied by a slightly younger man. Both
of them were dressed formally for the interview, in suits with
vests; very much two European gentlemen. Springmann told
us as we walked—he did not want to sit—about the information
on the new destruction camps that Oskar brought to the meeting in Budapest. To confer with Springmann, Oskar had smuggled himself into Budapest from Kraków in a railway truck full
of newspapers. He was very careful to be sure he had not been
followed to the rendezvous hotel, was anxious about listening
devices and, once inside, opened the door suddenly a few
times to catch potential eavesdroppers. Then he sat down and
began to speak to Springmann and his associate.

The death camps had been established, he told them. Belzec
was one of them, but there were new camps at Treblinka and

Maidanek and Sobibor too, and they were beginning the con-
struction of a new area at Auschwitz-Birkenau, which would be
the mother of camps. The SS were dissatisfied with the carbon
monoxide gassing, even though that method was capable of
killing thousands a day, and even though the commandant of
Belzec, Christian Wirth, was a great promoter of carbon monoxide. Other chemicals had, however, been tested with more
success. But whatever gas was used, disposal of corpses was a
big problem too.

It was the winter of 1942–43, Springmann told us in the
park, and the world knew something about the mass slaugh-
ters which were occurring under the Nazi regime, but he himself had been unaware, until Schindler spoke to him in that
hotel room in Budapest, of the technical experiments aimed
at mass extermination. In the early twenty-first century, we
are accustomed to the concept that these things happened in
World War II, but in 1942–43, to an outsider who had not
yet heard the tidings, what Schindler had to say would have
seemed like science fiction. Springmann, a German Jew, felt
himself an inheritor of a European identity as well as a Jewish
one. Could these things be envisaged and carried out by Germans?

While Oskar was briefly in Hungary, Springmann told us,
Sedlacek the dentist took him to dinner with a shady character
called Dr. Schmidt, the sort of man about whom Oskar was always very judgmental, just as he had been judgmental about
his own father. Oskar warned Sedlacek and Springmann that
they shouldn't give money for Jewish relief and rescue to

someone like Schmidt. Sedlacek remarked that there was an understanding that an operative could keep 10 percent of the money he was given, but Oskar, the enthusiastic black-marketeer, passionately disapproved of that.

Because the SS destruction system was so pervasive, so unlike anything else that had happened before in history, Springmann's noble operation could produce a merely partial salvation. Sometimes it was a matter of bribing an official to let an individual Jew live, or smuggling out a crucial figure with false papers. Oskar paid some tens of thousands of Springmann's funds to get a particular woman out of Montelupich Prison in Kraków and equipped with travel documents.

The heroic old man finished his story by saying he had had reunions with Oskar in the 1960s, and praising him as a whistle-blower.

Ten

Even in 1981, the road from Tel Aviv to Jerusalem was considered mildly dangerous, transporting people through former battlefields where the wreckage of tanks and trucks still lay beside the road. This had been the route Oskar had taken every year for a decade to meet his Jerusalem survivors, and it was also the track his corpse took to its burial place on Mount Zion in 1974. I was very pleased to be taking that road myself. Judy would be coming to Jerusalem in a day or so. Our teenage daughters were to be minded by my mother, loving but percipient, and by their overindulgent grandfather, who had spent time himself in Tel Aviv and Jerusalem during the war as an Australian soldier on leave from Egypt and Libya. My mother would not be susceptible to my daughters' excuses about avoiding school or study. Not to study, said my mother, was the same as stealing from your parents. I was delighted the girls would be exposed to such a vigorous message.

We were booked into the excellent King David Hotel, on the

western side of Jerusalem. I had first heard of the King David from my father—as an NCO, he had needed to borrow an Australian officer's uniform to get in there for a drink. Then, in 1946, during the British Mandate's rule in Palestine, at which time it housed many British officers, the Jewish underground had famously bombed it, killing ninety guests. I remember my father coming home from work with his *Daily Mirror*, and saying. "They've blown up the King David!"

Poldek had demanded rooms which looked directly out upon the walls of the ancient city. I could see the eighth-century Al-Aqsa Mosque, the glittering Dome of the Rock, and the Wailing Wall where Jews prayed to lament the final destruction of Solomon's Temple by the Roman emperor Titus.

Moshe Bejski, a distinguished moderate of the Israeli Supreme Court, a man who would write on issues of forgetting and forgiveness, who believed the survival of the Jewish state could not justify torture, and bemoaned later backsliding over justifiable compensation to former prisoners by the Swiss banks, had also been an eighteen-year-old prisoner in Oskar's Brinnlitz camp. His brother, who had been killed in the early Arab-Israeli conflict, had been in Oskar's Brinnlitz camp too. In the factory-camp, which produced no shells but was run almost entirely by the black-market operations of the Herr Direktor, Oskar would come to the young Bejski with German documents bearing official German stamps, and ask him if he could produce such a stamp. Oskar needed forged documents in order to move the merchandise he had acquired—liquor, cigarettes, fabric, food luxuries—up to Poland where they could be sold at a high price on the black market.

Bejski, a scholar, a man of serious intent and more than a little worried about the projected book, now warned me against accepting all of Poldek's exuberant tales unless they were corroborated by other prisoners. At the same time, he told his own fantastic but accurate stories. For example, he laughed and shook his head as he told the story of how he had been asked to make forged stamps for the documents which enabled Schindler to loot a bomb-damaged factory, Egyptsie Cigaretten, in Brno to the south of the Brinnlitz camp, and then ship the products by truck into Kraków. Bejski himself drove one of the trucks, and confessed that even he was astonished by the style with which Oskar sailed through the task of looting and then transporting the plunder for sale.

In his serene garden in Jerusalem, Bejski took me through all the documentation he had, which included many testimonies and a German magazine article on Oskar's motorbike racing career. By now I was acquiring a working knowledge of German and, with the help of dictionaries and grammar books, was able to translate this article into English for my own use, and the results are recorded (accurately, I hope and believe) in the pages on Oskar's motorbike craze which would appear in the book.

One of the more substantive documents Bejski had was a long copy—twenty to thirty foolscap pages, typed single-spaced—of a report Oskar wrote for the Joint Distribution Committee in 1957. In it, he accounted for the monies provided by Sedlacek from Jewish Relief and Rescue, and went on to what he had spent in his Kraków camp on extra food and SS bribes, then on maintaining his second camp, in Brinnlitz, and on the rescue of the Goleszów quarrymen who turned up half-dead on his doorstep.

Even Oskar's first Emalia camp at 4 Lipowa Street, Kraków, generously accommodated Jewish workers not only from Emalia, but from the box factory next door, the radiator plant and the garrison office. Since the required SS and Ukrainian guards came from Płaszów and were changed every two days, Emalia was not least a paradise because no guard had time to develop a grudge against any particular prisoner. Emalia also offered dignifying little mercies not permitted elsewhere. My Sydney friend Leosia Korn remembered that prisoners were allowed to heat up water on the surface of machinery, a luxury considered illegal in the SS-run workshops inside Płaszów. But mercy was also more direct. According to Dr. Biberstein, who worked in Emalia as a factory hand, the daily diet was roughly two thousand calories, as against half that in Płaszów.

Among other things in this document Bejski gave me, Schindler listed the amount paid to buy land from the parish priest of Brinnlitz for the burial of the dead among prisoners shipped from Goleszów. Apart from the standard payment owing to the SS—seven and a half reichsmarks each day per skilled worker and six RM per laborer—he claimed to have spent 1,800,000 zloty (U.S.$360,000) on food for the Emalia or DEF camp. None of his former prisoners disputed this estimate. He had also been forced to pay for the camp facilities at Brinnlitz and, before that, at Lipowa Street: the wire, the guards' huts, the installation of a delousing boiler in Brinnlitz, the daily food. Brinnlitz cost him U.S.$18,000 a week.

Reading this document, one is still amazed that he was able

to provide all this on such a scale that no one died of hunger or brutality. At the IG Farben Auschwitz-Monowitz plant alone, 25,000 prisoners—out of a workforce level maintained at 35,000—would die at their labor. Other reputable business-men in some of Germany's biggest businesses, including the great armament maker Krupp, and subsidiaries such as Ger-man Armament Works (DAW), also lost thousands of their workers through SS executions for supposed sabotage, and through beatings, starvation, overwork and disease. These were mainly young people originally in sustainable health at the time they were given the tattoo. By whatever means, Oskar reversed the rules and was able to keep most of the SS, except for inspectors, off the factory floor. Twenty-five years after publishing the book I finally wrote, I still respect his achieve-ment, and the fact that it consisted not merely in abstaining from evil but in the positive and expensive exercise of gen-erosity.

Josef Bau, a young draftsman and artist, had also had a hand in the forging of documents and stamps. He was one of the *Schindlerjuden*'s stars, like Ryszard Horowitz, in that he ac-quired an international reputation as an artist, especially for his terror-filled pen and ink drawings of the ghetto and Płaszów. His work seemed to say, "Look, here I am an artist, and the horror others brought to bear on me has kept me rooted there, under Amon Goeth's sniper rifle sights, in Płaszów, forever." His paintings are stark. He had never been able to escape into the fantastical cyber-universe where Ryszard worked against those laws of time and gravity which had kept him a child prisoner in Auschwitz.

In an improvised Jewish ceremonial in the women's huts, Bau had married a delicate girl named Rebecca. I was able to interview the Baus at their house in Jerusalem, and they seemed still to carry a camp pallor, and to be fragile, so that even Poldek spoke in a soft rumble in their presence, before the ornate, Eastern European–style tea party Rebecca Bau had set. One could see in Rebecca the beauty which had attracted Josef, and here they were, two edgy children of Płaszów, still consoling each other for the things they had seen. Bau had been a draftsman in Goeth's office and had needed to move about the camp, beholding as he walked, head down, many capricious savageries.

Though a visit to Oskar's grave was on our agenda, it was the sort of thing that got put off for interviews. Poldek and I at last went there the day before my wife's arrival, and it was a place I visited with her afterward. The Franciscan Church of the Dormition on Mount Zion is said to be near the site of the Last Supper, marking the place where the Apostles fell asleep when asked to keep a vigil with Christ. It was thus beautifully located, looking south over the Garden of Gethsemane, where Christ asked that he not be forced to drink his chalice of impending pain; then over the Valley of Gehenna, the garbage dump of ancient times and a synonym in the Bible for a burning hell; and finally over the Jordan, the far-off Dead Sea, and the austere, exquisite, naked mountains of Transjordan. Poldek and I reached the gates of the cemetery by the Franciscan church just after its closing time, but we called out to a Christian Arab watchman inside who approached the locked gate tentatively. Poldek indicated we would need the gates opened. Obviously a service fee would be required.

"I'll give him shekels," I whispered to Poldek, for I had a roll of notes in my pocket—courtesy, of course, of Poldek's Polish dealings.

"Shekels, shmekels!" growled Poldek. "He'll want dollars."

So once again I was wrong-footed on currency issues. Nonetheless, we entered the hillside cemetery and found, down the slope and to the east, Schindler's simple grave to which the Franciscans and the *Schindlerjuden* had led the corpse. The plain slab, apart from its bare Catholic iconography, mentioned little more than Oskar's birth and death dates. For a member of the Nazi Party, however, Schindler had managed to find himself a magnificent grave in Israeli ground crammed with symbols.

Much later, Spielberg would be similarly impressed with the place and use it in the film.

Then Judy was with us. As always when freed from household arm-wrestles over tidy rooms, etc., she became an organizer of our research effort on a scale even Poldek admired. He made kissing noises in her direction. "Mwah! Mwah! Darling, you are such a cutie and you know how things work."

"Better than me?" I asked.

"You're an innocent, but that's good sometimes!" He didn't specify how.

Judy is a good-humored, forthright woman who had come from the same background as myself—even down to the fact that one of her great-grandparents had been a political prisoner transported to Australia in the nineteenth century, as had one of my great-uncles from Newmarket in North Cork. She had already had an experience of Poldek's management and charm. Having been to Beverly Hills and made the mistake of calling it Los Angeles, she had been conducted by Poldek to one of the city limits where a sign announced its welcome to the city of Beverly Hills. Poldek gave her his standard lecture. "Beverly Hills is its own city with its own police and sanitation and fire brigade. Welcome to California, Beverly Hills!"

She had attended an event at one of the larger LA synagogues, at which Poldek insisted, against her own wishes, that she be given a place of honor. To each successive VIP marshal, he made a speech about the forthcoming book and her eminence as my wife! Thus she found herself sitting between the peace activist Tom Hayden and Governor Jerry Brown of California. She knew from that experience that Poldek could organize anything, whether it was necessary to do so or not.

Each morning, Judy and I caught the bus to the Yad Vashem, the monument itself and its library of archives. The buses seemed to be full of students—and soldiers, male and female, with semiautomatics. We would get off near the Avenue of the Righteous where in 1963 a tree had been planted in honor of Oskar and Emilie. Camera footage shot at Oskar's requiem mass in the Church of the Dormition was available at Yad Vashem, but much more than that.

Among the testimonies in Polish and English in the extensive Schindler archive were ones I would mention in the book, minority reports more or less, written by the father and son of a Kraków Jewish family, prewar owners of a hardware company, who had entered into a business arrangement with Oskar, putting up capital for Emalia in return for supplies of the product. Both father and son claimed that in 1940 Oskar had beaten them up during a physical dispute over merchandise. Oskar's own complaint against them was that they arrived at the loading dock of Emalia and bullied the workers into loading unauthorized amounts of enamelware. Their argument was that the quantities had already been agreed upon. Even though the father and son remained under Oskar's care in Brinnlitz, they never forgot their earlier disagreement. I spoke about these documents with Bejski, and also with Poldek. With varying degrees of emphasis—Poldek with raucous affront on behalf of his friend Schindler, and Bejski in a more measured way—both complained about the family in question, and neither of them thought it unlikely that Oskar had thrown some punches. "But after all," said Bejski, "Schindler saved their lives!"

When Schindler decided that he was going to make a second camp in Czechoslovakia after the closure of the Lipowa Street factory, a list of his current workers was assembled by Stern and others and sent off to Płaszów. There, sadly, it fell into the hands of a Jewish clerk named Marcel Goldberg, who is notorious among survivors for having said that it would take jewels to get on the list. My friend Poldek offered a bottle of vodka—presented to him by a guilt-stricken SS NCO, the same one who had begun by beating him—and it helped get himself and

Misia on the list. But the truth was that between the list prepared by Schindler and his people, and the one ultimately drawn up over several drafts by Marcel Goldberg, there was a difference; and some of Schindler's original workers, in their testimonies in Yad Vashem, blamed Oskar when they found themselves sent somewhere crueler—Mauthausen, for example.

I was fascinated to find these further potential flaws in the man, and knew that the contrary account of father and son needed to be included to round out the picture of Oskar—not that either Bejski or Poldek spent any time trying to dissuade me from doing so.

Due to the influence of Moshe Bejski and the insistence of Poldek, who kept on announcing to the Yad Vashem archivists that we were about to produce the book, the chief archivist gave us a special dispensation to take documents back to the hotel with us for copying. Scholarly women were flattered on their bone structure by Poldek, and scholarly men were blinded by his power of reminiscence of the towns and villages their grandfathers had come from in Poland. Judy went through the newspaper archives and made notes from them, and spent hours transcribing my tapes in the business center at the hotel. The names she transcribed took on a mythic dimension in our minds, so that when we met a particular Schindler prisoner, his or her record and general tale were known to us, and we felt we were meeting a legendary figure.

In between spates of work, Judy and I wandered around the old city on our own, knelt in the Church of the Holy Sepulchre, inside a minute oil lamp–lit chapel within the church which my father had visited on a World War II Australian air force jaunt from Egypt, and were blessed many times by a fervent old Coptic priest.

A **photocopying bill** arrived at our door one morning. It was not exorbitant, and Judy and I entered the lift to go down and pay it. Already about was Poldek, whose room was on the floor above.

After morning compliments, he asked, "You have an invoice there?"

Judy told him it was a bill for all the photocopying of documents, Bejski's and Yad Vashem's.

"They sent you an *invoice*?" he asked incredulously.

"Yes, and it's pretty reasonable too," I told Poldek. Indeed, a few such invoices for earlier copying had arrived at our door, and I had simply paid them.

"They can't ask you to pay. What are they thinking? Judy darling, let me see the invoice."

I said, "Listen, Poldek, it's fine. I'm looking after this."

Judy had no choice but to show him the invoice.

"Come with me to the desk," he ordered us as the lift reached the ground floor.

We argued, but our reasoning was washed away by the full tide of his outrage. We followed him to the front desk. My wife was better at handling him than I was, but I believe she came along to see the show—Poldek in action. He presented the bill as if it were something that had slipped through a gap in management's general omniscience. I watched a pale Ashkenazi reception clerk bend over the desk patiently to look at the bill Poldek presented to his gaze and say, "That's right, Mr. Pfefferberg. You see, we copied . . . at so many shekels per ten pages . . ."

Poldek growled, stood back and adopted the sort of pose rarely seen in those days except on opera stages and old newsreels of vanished potentates. He pointed heavenward. It should have been ridiculous, except for the authority of his rage, the certainty of his vision.

"One day," he said, "there will be a plaque over this reception desk, and it will say that here Thomas Keneally and Leopold Pfefferberg researched the story of Oskar Schindler and his *Schindlerjuden*! And you want to charge us for lousy photostatic copies? Can you imagine what my friend Justice Moshe Bejski of the Israeli Supreme Court would think of that?"

I stood some yards behind Poldek, and would, in my timorous Gentile way, have been happy to pay the bill and end the dramatics right there. But a duty manager arrived to reason with Poldek, looking as optimistic as an uninformed conscript going into battle against elite troops. He could not match the hypnotic conviction of which Poldek was capable. Poldek *could see* the coming plaque above the desk. The bill was, to my acute discomfort, forgiven us, and no one in the business office bothered sending us photocopying invoices anymore.

Toward the end of our stint in Yad Vashem I watched the archival film of Oskar's German television documentary, filmed in Frankfurt not long before his death. Oskar spoke in a profound rumble in which cognac and cigars had induced an attractive rawness. When asked about his motivation, he spoke of "fellow feeling and compassion" for people who were being treated with "brutality you could not imagine." Long-faced, balding and overcoated, one could well imagine that face belonging both to hero and criminal, masking a thousand sins and generosities. In other words, his face seemed to me very European, a face that could have fitted splendidly on a landgrave or freebooter in a painting of some important incident during the Thirty Years' War.

We had accumulated a mass of material. Poldek planned to go on to Italy and Hong Kong to buy new stock for his warehouse and the Handbag Studio. By now, of course, he was well-known to the hotel staff, a terror to the front desk, a friend to other guests, a generous fellow to the Sephardic maids. When Poldek took his place in one of the so-called charabancs, Mercedes cars which ran passengers down to Tel Aviv, he wept and wished us well. "We are brothers to the grave!" he asserted.

Yet there was something in Judy and me which yelped with relief when his car drove away through the garden of the King David down to the road. We would not be worked so hard now! We had a holiday of three days before we had to go to Tel Aviv ourselves.

It was a relief to do more normal things. We took a long bus trip, down past Qumran, and the caves in the cold and arid hills where the Dead Sea Scrolls were found. We climbed Masada, scene of a mass suicide of Israeli Zealots, men, women and children who were about to be overrun by the Romans. The Roman engineering works and ramps were visible to us and sad in their mute acknowledgment that the capture of Masada had availed the generals little in the long run. The remaining quarters and the ritual baths atop Masada gave immediacy to the lives of the Jews who once held out there.

I wondered why ancient fundamentalist sects were often historically revered. There was some justification for the mass suicide on Masada, since the Zealots believed that they would be put to the sword, their wives misused and slaughtered, their children sold into slavery. Their actions had thus become part of the Israeli myth, even though many urbane Israelis nonetheless despised modern fundamentalism, and all the more so for its power in modern Israeli politics.

We bathed in the Dead Sea, as my father had. Hiring a car—an exercise of considerable expense in Israel to this day—we went along the coast to the remarkable Roman port of Caesarea and to the crusaders' port of Acre, on up to the Golan Heights, past many a kibbutz, and then down to Galilee.

Briefly back in Tel Aviv, I saw the Dresners for the last time, and took Judy for a meal in what we thought of as Oskar's Romanian restaurant. Then, with our mass of tapes and transcripts and photocopies, we set off to Greece and Australia. The Zakopanean ice pick survived both Greek and Australian customs, and holding it in my hand I made, fairly enough, an object of amusement for my teenage daughters; the bewildered father returned with strange implements from overly portentous adventures.

Eleven

Our house at the beach, and my downstairs office, proved a good place to write a book on the Holocaust. Looking down the slope I could see each day, from the pool table on which I spread all the documents, surfboard riders born long after the cataclysm, children to whom Hitler was a mere rumor. I had so much material to stock my awesome tale, and the great thing about the mass of research documents was that they convinced me the writing of the book would be easy. There was also that certain obsession from which writers suffer—that somehow the world needs to hear this story. The writer is the ancient mariner who distracts the guests at the wedding feast, and is hell-bent on wrenching their imaginations in a direction they had not necessarily intended to take them.

Like many writers, I thought that I could tell this story swiftly, without being influenced by it at a profound, partially disabling level. That is ever the writer's dream—to be a raider, straight in, straight out, leaving none of one's soul behind as hostage. So I did not expect a chaos of dreams, I did not expect to be myself a target for Amon Goeth's querulous, malign spirit.

Even so, Schindler would be the context for everything that happened, his career the lens through which everything was seen. I had decided that long ago, as a trick to give the book its unity. But it was much easier to propose up-front these tricks of narration than it was to fulfill them in reality. Poldek did what he could. He kept on calling and promising me that when the book was published I would win "the Novell Prize—I've already booked my seat to Oslo!"

"It's Stockholm, Poldek."

"Well, Stockholm. You mark my words."

There were two weeks of utter despair in the middle of the writing, when I thought that I had lost my grasp of the material, and felt that the resources, imaginative and financial, I had put into the project had certainly been wasted. This is a common midbook experience for writers, but I took it all the more seriously in this case because of what I thought of as the gravity of the material, the gravity of the story. I knew that if I lost the capacity to tell this tale, I might be so damaged by defeat that it would be the end of me as a writer. With the added horror of having to find some $40,000, already expended, to compensate Simon & Schuster.

I found, too, that even in Australia people had set attitudes to the Holocaust. The old complaint came up about the Jews having been too passive. I remember ungraciously throwing my credit card at a friend who took the line of "They sold each other out," and raging out of a restaurant. Not only was this a parody of the truth, but, as in so many cases of historic oppression, the Nazi system was designed to exploit collaboration. As if there hadn't been French who sold out, and Ukrainians, and millions of others. My friend's opinion, based merely on meeting Jewish clients in the rag trade, implied that I didn't know any of this and needed enlightenment. Goldberg had sold out some on the list, the *Judenräte* sold out individuals. Were the Jews to be different from every other human subjugated race and behave with an inhuman perfection?

Anyhow, doubting the project, I had recourse to whiskey. There was a heater in my office and, blurred and depressed on a day of gales, I dropped beside it and slept. My folders of transcripts and documents lay heaped on the pool table. I had divided them into chronological dossiers. One dossier was labeled *Oskar—Childhood*, another *Oskar—Young Manhood*, then *Adult Oskar to 1939*. The others were named for portions of years and major events, including *Oskar—Escape to the West*, *Oskar to 1957*, *Oskar to 1974*. All this lush remembrance and these supporting documents were wasted on me that day. After a time, my wife entered the office to see how I was, saw me at what could politely be called "rest," and—though I didn't know my eyes were still partly open—was gratified to see that the anguish of the past couple of days had now given way to exhaustion.

I have since felt the need to apologize to my wife and daughters for such episodes. They rebuff the apologies with some amusement. I accuse them of being in denial; it was nasty and they were entitled to say so. Guilt persists over the times I have imposed my anguish about the progress of a book upon the household.

Before my crash, I had reached the stage when Oskar, having set up his factory in Lipowa Street, has acquired Jewish workers. One morning, after heavy sleep, it was all at once possible to begin again. It was possible to narrate in a manner which placed the reader within the chaotic and fearful experience of prisoners. The documents, the memories of individuals, became vivid to me again. Why does the capacity to write seem to suddenly vanish so utterly from a writer, and then so thoroughly return? It's as if the conscious brain had to be disabled to allow all the sorting, classifying, arranging and selection that derives from the unconscious. In any case, the dangerous interlude was over.

One factor that prevented my total disappearance into the book was that my days were enlivened and redeemed by demands from my daughters—for help with interpretation of a poem set for homework, a request that they be driven here or there in Sydney, or driven to school when through artful delay it became too late for them to catch the bus. They had the normal teenage desire not to be associated with their unfashionable parents, and frequently asked not to be taken to the front of the school. But as intense as their sibling fights could be, it was Judy's and my good fortune that they had not gone through any thoroughgoing alienation from their parents which characterized many adolescents we knew, and which created chronic conflict in some homes. There were few slammed doors and few attempts to destroy the souls of parents in our house by the Pacific, and Judy and I always considered that the purest good luck. Sometimes it must have seemed as though I was the only child to be dealt with. And to start the day, however unwillingly, with an outing became a useful form of mental refreshment.

Another diversion was that my younger daughter and I followed the local rugby league team, Manly-Warringah, in those days perhaps the most famous of all Australian teams and the most resented. Every game day at Brookvale Oval, we took our position behind the goalposts, she fully clothed in team colors and waving a massive maroon and white flag. At such moments I was far removed from the Holocaust, and the pernicious referee was always a vastly more minor villain than Amon Goeth. Thus an Australian winter passed and the team kept winning, to be defeated by the Parramatta Eels (*Parramatta*, or *Burramatta*, meaning "the Place of the Eels" in the Aboriginal tongue of the Sydney basin). The Eels, sadly, had the best backline in the history of the game.

And amid all the concern about team injuries and the perfidy of referees and the suddenness with which other teams could spring ambushes, the written tale took on substance. I had always been the sort of writer who writes an entire draft of a book, from start to finish, then returns to it and rewrites it entirely again, and then again. At that stage I had not acquired a computer, so that I wrote everything in longhand, then dictated it, with punctuation marks included, onto tape. The tapes were typed up by a woman named Barbara who ran an office service in Avalon, a beachside suburb near ours. By the warm December of 1981 she was already typing parts of the earliest, rough version.

When the whole thing was done, and I had the complete typescript from her, I began rewriting in longhand, totally reworking or rejecting the passages which did not pass muster but retaining the sections of the typescript which were still usable, making corrections on them, and then gluing the new handwritten revised sections to the surviving fragments of the typescript. I ended up with huge screeds, rather like Roman scrolls, stiffened, typescript-to-longhand, by glue. This was then typed again by Barbara, given a final edit and occasional rewrite, and served as a first draft. It went off to the publishers in Britain and America, maybe a little under a year after Poldek and I had set out on our research journey.

Complicated publishing events had in the meantime occurred in America. Nan Talese, the editor who had put up the advance for Schindler and had been enthusiastic about the book, had left Simon & Schuster to take a higher post elsewhere. It is always disappointing for a writer when the commissioning editor departs, since it can be touch-and-go whether the new editor will be imbued with a similar affection for the project. The editor who inherited me was Patricia Solomon. She did everything we could have asked, but could not influence the scale of the print run—the numbers of copies printed, that is. That was my impression, in any case; publishing is a business in which editors often keep the truth of such issues from the writer for the sake of politeness, a desire to avoid conflict, or a kind wish not to bruise the author's ego.

There is a strange stillness in a writer's household after a book has been posted off. The atmosphere is a little like that of a school the day after breakup. The research is idly packed into boxes, and the reference books put in their own section of the shelves, some of them never to be consulted again.

The reactions of Patricia Solomon and my UK editor, Ion Trewin, to the book were positive. But the fact that Nan Talese, the initial enthusiast, was gone remained a shadow over it. In those days I had not reached the sort of maturity which I have tried to achieve in later life. The beginning of sanity for a writer is to see the beloved work as an item on a conveyor, a listing in a catalogue, holding a position, probably not too high a position, in the plans of a publisher who has a season's worth of books to produce and sell to the public. The woman who would be, as its commissioner, its best advocate was through no fault of hers missing from that whole process. The writer should simply celebrate the miracle that someone as plain as most of us are could have produced anything halfway worth reading. But seeing things that way is a hard thing to do if the writer depends on the book for his living and for a measure of who he is.

A dear New York friend of mine, Irv Bauer, was then enthusiastically promoting one of my failed plays, *Bullie's House*. It was about the plunder of holy totemic items from Aboriginals. It was as predictably wordy as any novelist's play, but Irv loved that. Plays were incarnations of ideas to him, and a wealth of ideas could justify some lack of technique. Judy and I went from Sydney to New York for the workshopping of the play at New Dramatists in an old church in Hell's Kitchen.

We were to occupy a flat at the top of the studio, a lonely place at night, when the entire building was darkened except for our little hutch. A Hell's Kitchen local, employed because, as a reformed thief, he was good at retrieving stolen items (including New Dramatists' coffeemaker), would knock on our door about ten-thirty every night to check that we were well.

It was during this journey that the Simon & Schuster legal department got to work on the dramatis personae of the book. They wanted all the former associates of Schindler and *Schindlerjuden* mentioned in the book to sign a legal release. They wanted me to seek a release even from SS men who had long since died or migrated to remote places—maybe Australia, Canada, Argentina. And they sought and got a release from Mrs. Schindler as well, based on what I had written about her part in the rescue.

To help ensure that these releases of the former prisoners and the many others were signed, I enlisted the help of Poldek again, whom we had seen in California on the way through to New York from Sydney. Schindler's lawyer, Irving Glovin, also helped, though he was a little edgy at the way the raucous, riotous, subversive aspect of Oskar had been depicted. To him the question was still the nature of altruism, as if it were almost a glandular, chemical entity. Glovin called the British and American publishers for reassurance. Poldek rang them to ask them in detail what their plans for publication were, and to urge them along. In any case, thanks to Poldek, the clearances drawn up by Simon & Schuster's lawyers were signed.

In this period, too, I met up again with Oskar's former lover, Ingrid, and her husband, and made a last attempt to organize an interview—since there was still time to write a few things into the book—with a very successful shipping executive who was a Schindler survivor, and indeed had been one of the younger prisoners who escaped westward with Poldek in the small hours of the first morning of peace. He was sympathetic to the project, but very tense about being asked to revisit the pain of those years. Poldek was, of course, dismissive of the man's decision, but I could by now sympathize with his reluctance. It was not a matter of ingratitude, as Poldek perceived it, but trepidation at opening the box of disabling horror. The man did not want to look back and be ossified by what he saw.

Poldek was coming through New York on his way to Italy and Hong Kong to buy leather goods for his wholesale business and the store. He insisted on meeting the urbane Patricia Solomon at Simon & Schuster. Patricia was eager to have the meeting since she had heard all my Poldek stories. First of all, Poldek praised Patricia's features, the old bone structure stuff. It was surprisingly not a tiresome act. Then he told her I was fussy when he mentioned the "Novell Prize" and asked her to convince me we were bound to win it with this book. "Oh, possibly," Patricia indulged him. "Simon & Schuster publishes many Nobel Prize contenders."

He seemed appeased. Then he asked her how many copies she would print for the first run.

She replied, "Somewhere around thirty-three to thirty-five thousand copies. This is in hardcover."

"Only thirty-five thousand? Patricia, my darling, you're going to need more than that. Print one hundred and fifty thousand copies and they'll go in a week."

"Hardcover?" asked Patricia.

"Of course, hardcover," said Poldek, from the depths of his expertise in the publishing industry. "You'll be a legend by the next weekend. Your bosses will love you, and why shouldn't they? Beauty and brains!"

His hopeful prophecy would in fact prove closer to what the demand would be, though it would certainly take more than a mere week to sell that number. He did not understand that the decision would not have been made by Patricia alone. Patricia laughed nervously, and I wished Poldek would just stop extolling the book.

"We can always go back to print," she said.

This was an assurance publishers often gave, but in those days going back to print meant three lost weeks. When writers meet in bars, they always trade horrifying tales of a book's momentum stalled when the first printing was snapped up early because of radiant reviews, and the second printing came too late to revive the initial impact.

Dan Green, Simon & Schuster's head of publishing, had made his repute by publishing Arnold Schwarzenegger's *Pumping Iron* and *The Jane Fonda Workout Book*. He took an unexpected stand on the title of the book. I had suggested two titles—*Schindler's Ark* and *Schindler's List*—indicating to Ion Trewin in London that I liked *Ark* better than *List*. It was not only the question of evoking Noah's Ark, but also the Ark of the Covenant, a symbol of the contract between Yahweh and the tribe of Israel. A similar though very rough compact existed between Oskar and his people. If they did their work properly—if the accountant kept the books well, if the engineers and the people on the floor produced, or, later in the war, if they *appeared* to be producing for the sake of covering his black-market operations—then he would rescue them. I call it a "rough compact" because of those people who were lost to the list through factors Schindler could not control. His behavior in regard to the three hundred women sent to Auschwitz, however, indicates that in all probability he did what he could to keep his list intact.

Patricia now took us along to see Dan Green himself. He was an athletic-looking man and seemed to have benefited from the advice of Arnold himself. He adopted something of a tough-guy air. He raised the issue of the title.

"I've discussed it with the Brits," I told him. "Hodder's are going with *Schindler's Ark* rather than *Schindler's List*. And I prefer *Ark* too."

Green said that it was impossible to have *Ark*. I asked him why. He said that American Jewry was very sensitive to the accusation that the Jews had been somehow passive in the face of their destruction. And *Ark* implied passivity, the prisoners entering two by two.

I told him there was no way that I wanted to offend Jewish people in America, but the issue had not been raised in Britain. He said the Jewish community in Britain was more diffuse, less focused on apparent slights.

"But what about the Ark of the Covenant?" I asked. "The idea that there had been a covenant between Schindler and his people?"

"No," said Green. "People wouldn't get that. They'd only get this passive thing, and see it as a slur."

For once Poldek didn't have an opinion. As long as they printed one hundred and fifty thousand copies as a first print run, he was happy, and that was his objective with Dan Green. "It is the great story of humanity man to man," as his mantra went and as he now told Green. "You're printing too few. But whatever you call it, you and Thomas should subtitle it *A Great Story of Humanity Man to Man*."

Green thought that such a subtitle was "clunky," and I had already told Poldek as much. I argued with Green, though, that the British proofs were about to arrive at my place in Australia, and that as soon as I got home I had to correct them. Not only that, but the book had already appeared in Hodder's autumn catalogue as *Schindler's Ark*. A change now was impossible for them. Naturally, Pat Solomon did not buy into my debate with Green, but I could see that what British publishers were doing was always something of a minor matter with their Manhattan counterparts.

In between arguments with Green, I asked a few of the Jewish kids, young playwrights and directors who hung around

New Dramatists in Hell's Kitchen, whether they would be offended by the title Dan Green abominated. They had certainly
heard of the issue: the accusation of some supposed endemic
passivity in Jews was raised by many Gentiles. Others, including Poldek, were not so fussed.

After a week, rightly or wrongly, I consented to Green's
proposition. I did not have quite Poldek's scale of confidence
in the story. I certainly had no sense that this would be my
best-known book, and that the two-title issue would haunt me
and generate questions for the next twenty years and more.
Ultimately, I thought that I couldn't take the risk of offending
American Jewry, not only because I wanted to sell them books,
but also for Green's reasons. And I had other things to concentrate on, being still busy with legal and other matters. I had
also sent the full text for correction to Poldek, Pemper, Bejski,
Mrs. Stern and the Dresners. I had sent sections of the text to
the Fagens, the Korns, the Rosners, the Horowitzes, Dr.
Schindel, and so on. I would incorporate their corrections.

Now came the question of whether the book should be cate-
gorized as fiction in the Library of Congress classification system. For both commercial reasons and reasons of passion, I
didn't want this book stuck in that section against the back wall
of most American bookstores labeled JUDAICA. Books classified
as such are often splendid works, but I feared that Gentiles
might feel they need not apply. Poldek agreed with me on that.
I felt that in Schindler I had written as a novelist, with a novelist's narrative pace and graphicness, though not in the sense of
a fictionalizer. If three or four people told me that Schindler

had more or less said certain things, I certainly put them in quotation marks, but otherwise the manuscript was largely innocent of dialogue.

Dan Green agreed on this proposition. People would ever afterward ask why it was classified as fiction—apparently deniers would later point to that classification to undermine the book's clear faith in the Holocaust's reality. I was convinced at the time that this "documentary novel" qualified as fiction, though was at the extreme end of the phylum or genus. I might have made both of these decisions the same way if I had them to make again, but I would certainly not defend them to the death.

Twelve

The final legal permissions and revisions of the book were done, and Judy and I left our perch in Hell's Kitchen and flew back to the stillness of Sydney's Bilgola Beach, impinged upon merely by the noisy traffic of waves.

My mother and father, as we so automatically expected, had done a splendid job looking after the girls.

By the end of the process of reediting according to the notes of sundry associates of Oskar, I had got to become friends by correspondence and telephone calls with genial Ion Trewin, the editor at Hodder's. I could tell from his letters that he was one of those Englishmen who were passionate about writing, and who also loved cricket as an art form—indeed, when I got to know him and his broad, piratical, bearded features in person, I would see he generally wore a Lords Cricket Ground member's tie, when not wearing the tie of the Garrick Club, which was frequented by actors, publishers and newspapermen (no women). He appeared to me a good blend of artist and British establishment.

As the book neared its October 1982 publication in Britain, I heard from Ion that on the basis of the proofs, it had been short-listed for the Booker Prize. This is the premier British literary prize, for which writers from all over the Commonwealth can be nominated. Hodder's considered *Schindler* to belong to the species Novel, had submitted it, and the book had now been short-listed. I had had three earlier books of mine short-listed, so I didn't think there was much danger of winning the thing, especially given what one could call the genre uncertainty of the book. When I told Poldek, he took the news calmly. "There you are, Thomas. What did I tell you? What did I tell you?"

The Booker had become so renowned in part because of a literary scandal, an attack the prolific and ever-entertaining Anthony Burgess had made on it two years previously. I was in London for a book tour at the time, and had had to do some editing in a suite at the BBC, the Shepherd's Bush studio, of a documentary I had made for a series named *Writers and Places*. I had been formed by two localities—the Sydney suburb of Homebush, in which I had spent my late childhood and adolescence, and the Macleay Valley, four hundred kilometers north, in which I had spent early childhood, and which had always had a very strong impact on my writing.

Another writer was in the editing suite that evening, also involved in a final edit of his *Writers and Places* segment. It was Anthony Burgess, who came with his Maltese wife and a satchel of Tiger Beer, the beer of Singapore, to honor the impact that city-state had had on his writing career. He was in robust form, and told us that later that evening he would appear on television with William Golding, who had won the 1980 Booker Prize ahead of Burgess's own brilliant book, *Earthly Powers*. He considered Golding's book, *Rites of Passage*, the third part of a trilogy about a voyage to Australia in the nineteenth century, effete by the standards of Golding's earlier work, which included *Lord of the Flies* and *Pincher Martin*.

So, after we had worked for a while on the Steinbeck editing machines with our producer, Burgess *did* descend to a studio at Television House where he made his robust denunciation. That controversy seemed to be stoked far more by Burgess than it was responded to by Golding, but like all literary brawls it drew considerable attention, and irrationally added to the mystique of the Booker as a prize which caused some people to read all short-list contenders and take passionate positions on this book or that, often positions undercut by the jury's final decision. By the time the glamorous young writer Salman Rushdie won the prize in 1981 for *Midnight's Children*, it had become more than a literary event, with notable British actors reading segments from the short-listed novels on awards night, and Ladbrokes betting agency running a book on the result.

Flown to London both to promote *Schindler's Ark* and to attend the 1982 Booker dinner, I discovered with astonishment that *Ark* was firming up as second favorite at Ladbrokes. What fatuity for a book on life and death, heaven and hell. My price was 7–2, but the splendid William Boyd's *An Ice-Cream War* was the favorite.

I began to see the new importance of the Booker when Ion Trewin collected me from the quaint but wonderful Basil Street Hotel in Knightsbridge to take me out to sign books around town. The bookstores each had a table with the books of the six short-listed writers on it. The playwright John Arden's *Silence Among the Weapons*, Lawrence Durrell's *Constance, or Solitary Practices*. Alice Thomas Ellis, the fey contributor to *The Spectator*, had a book named *The 27th Kingdom*, which no one, including her exuberantly ironic self, expected to win. Then there was Boyd's *An Ice-Cream War*, and Timothy Mo's *Sour Sweet*. Tim Mo was perhaps the first notable Anglo-Chinese writer, and his book, which I began to read, was complex and engaging. I could not imagine the quasi-novel *Schindler's Ark* succeeding over it. To be nominated had itself become a mechanism for selling books.

I was a little bemused to find out, though, that I would need a dinner suit for the Booker evening at the Guild Hall. But Moss Bros, the traditional London outfitters, were very kind and exacting in that regard. I went to Ladbrokes and put fifty pounds on the nose of William Boyd, and a smaller sum, which my wife had given me, on myself. On awards night, as Ion and I both detoured for a safety urination in the Guild Hall toilets downstairs, my Moss Bros rented dinner suit didn't look too inferior to Ion's own, which, by the jaunty bulge at his waistband, I judged he might have had since his university days.

A famous Australian-born publisher, Carmen Callil, one of the judges, came up to me as I entered the glittering dining room with its escutcheons and wonderful stained glass, and gave me a vague message that I took as a mere compliment. She said later it was a coded message that I'd won, but if so, I was unable to interpret it as such. I felt no sickening tension as we sat at our tables, though my English agent, Tessa Sayle, was breathless with hope. Despite being an Austrian baroness connected to the Hapsburgs, Tessa had always had a soft spot for Australians in general, and Australian clients. She had been married to an Australian named Murray Sayle, a renowned *London Times* journalist, and the breakup of the marriage didn't seem to diminish her enthusiasm for the outrageous and sometimes unconsciously inappropriate things Australians were likely to say among the British.

The dinner began in culinary splendor, and it was not until afterdinner drinks that the BBC Two producer gave us our instructions as an audience and the television show started—Derek Jacobi reading a segment from *Schindler's Ark* and other actors reading segments from the other short-listed novels. Dessert and then calvados were served, and I opportunistically drank Ion's, seeing that he was much too nervous. I was happy to have met and to be in the company of renowned Londoners. I was content to have seen the dazzling interior of the Guild Hall. The Stoics would have been proud of my repose of soul.

When a fashionably stammering Professor John Carey read out my name from the rostrum, I felt momentarily electrocuted by an electric pulse of disbelief as direct as an arrow. Walking forward with a dazed half-smile on my face and two glasses of calvados the worse, I remember at the rostrum commending the judges for the recklessness of the great mistake

they had just made. I thanked Poldek, not only for his merchandise, I said, but for the wonderful tale he had harbored
and then surrendered to me. As I descended for interviews,
there was barely time to caress Ion and Tessa Sayle before I was
taken by a phalanx of Booker-minders to a press conference. I
said an occasional daring thing, such as that, being the first
Australian to have won the Booker, I hoped it was the beginning of the death of *our* cultural cringe and *their* cultural contempt. I was asked to defend *Schindler's Ark*'s claim to be a
novel. It must be, I said, opting out perhaps too cutely, because
the judges thought so, and who am I to argue with them? But
the controversy was well away by the next afternoon's papers,
and would not cease for some time. Like most controversy, it
initiated a frenzy of interest in the book.

When, late on that night of the award, Ion and I got back to
the Basil Street Hotel for the last thoughtful drink of the day,
the bar was closed.

I did not sleep. While I was breakfasting in the Basil Street's
wonderful restaurant, one which would have suited Henry
James, I was called away to answer the phone. It was the Australian actor Bryan Brown, who had been with me in Sorrento
two years before. He had also acted in *The Chant of Jimmie
Blacksmith*, and was having success at that time through the
miniseries *A Town Like Alice*. As did many Australians, he saw
all these Australian phenomena as strikes against our cultural
ignominy. "Isn't it great," he asked me, "when two boys from
the western suburbs really rip it up the Poms?" I felt that perhaps this attitude took no account of the fact that a British jury

had generously chosen me, but at the same time I shared in Bryan's felon delight.

I was still prodigiously awake at ten that morning. I sat in the hotel's living room, where I had a scheduled interview with a journalist from the *Irish Times*. Her name was Maeve Binchy, and she'd already had a manuscript accepted by Hodder. Indeed, she would become an outrageously successful writer of fiction. But for the moment she saw herself as the supplicant journalist, which bespoke her Irish no-nonsense, no-airs ways. She thanked me for not having canceled the interview now that I was, as she said, "a rock star." In the Basil Street's lounge, full of its chinoiserie, she murmured to me, "It's late in the day." She waved a hand at a waiter. It was just after ten. "Do you think they'd mind if we had whiskey in our tea?" Maeve Binchy and I became friends for life. She often holidayed in Australia, she told me, because her English husband, Gordon Snell, who worked for Irish radio and television, RTÉ, had spent years there after he was evacuated from Singapore as a boy.

I had lived a limited life as a youth, and my naivety was largely unpracticed. It was only arduously, and through extensive travel, that I had become anything approaching a man of the world. With Maeve and others, I showed my colonial lack of class by not disapproving of the Booker's hoopla, which is the de rigueur pose of anyone destined to win it. "It's all nonsense, it's all a lottery, it makes the book no better than it was yesterday." It is fashionable for writers to despise the prize till they are short-listed, and from there on to declare the whole exercise crass and, as some argued, rather like a beauty contest. But no one ever turned down his short-listing, though one admirable winner, John Berger, donated his prize to the industrial struggle of the West Indians who worked on the Booker McConnell sugar plantations. And no writer, as far as I know, ever withdrew his nomination from the Booker short list.

At home in Sydney, Judy heard in the small hours of the morning from a neighbor who came rushing down our street, crying out that the ABC news said I had won.

For Poldek, this was the validation of his belief that this story was for Gentiles. He showed it by giving away a signed copy of the book with every purchase of goods in the Handbag Studio over one hundred dollars. The question about whether the book was a novel or not raged on, but every morning new stocks of the book, printed the day before and rushed up from Kent, cluttered the marble lobbies of Hodder's beautiful eighteenth-century headquarters in Bedford Square. Salesmen got there early so that they could pick up enough copies to satisfy the bookshops they served. What a heady and extremely rare time for a writer, when demand could not quite be satisfied!

I remember a glorious, boozy press-and-publishing bash in the back garden of the old Bedford Square house. But behind the celebration there lay the reality that this book was built on the blood of innocents. I went on suffering a merited and intimate nightmare, perhaps fueled by an excess of celebratory wine and spirits, of Amon Goeth selecting me from a line of prisoners for some unspecified death. The taste one gets of death in dreams I find more penetrating and atmospheric than the ordinary fear one might suffer while awake.

In the following week I was called on as if a Londoner to perform civic duties—to open a new library in the City of London, for example. I wondered if I should tell them about my Irish Republican great-uncle, who was sentenced to transportation to Western Australia for sedition. Or my Uncle Johnny, who had come to London on rowdy Australian leave from the Western Front and fallen in love with a Scottish nurse in 1917, an ardor from which nothing developed.

Now, laden with accidental renown, I flew back to Australia. Judy organized a wonderful welcome party. The tension between Bookerdom and the knowledge that my work had benefited from testimonies from people who had suffered extremities of terror made me frequently but privately uneasy, and Judy understood this. Yet there was undeniable joy in the homecoming, and acceptance among my own. I was above all grateful for the excitement my teenage daughters felt over what had happened. They didn't adopt any air of adolescent boredom at all.

Thirteen

Writers always complain about American tours. There is only one thing worse than your American publisher sending you out, city to city, condemning you to flights at 5:30 a.m. or else 11:05 p.m., and that is if your American publisher doesn't care enough about the book to make you do it. The size of the United States, the proliferation of big cities, and the fact that early morning and late night television and radio were so popular in America, helped squeeze the writer's available rest time. It is an experience full of semivivifying showers before the sun rises, and drinking grainy black coffee in departure lounges.

Simon & Schuster were publishing the book as *Schindler's List*, in accordance with my earlier lost quarrel with Dan Green, and though they went back to print even before publication, based on the reaction of the booksellers, I found by the start of the third week of the tour that, as Poldek had predicted, they had sold out. I was expatiating on radio and TV into vacancy. I complained to Patricia Solomon, and informed

Poldek of the sad fact. He did his *What-did-I-tell-you?* act with Patricia.

Out in California in mid-tour, I saw Poldek and the lawyer Glovin, Poldek omnisciently predicting that the next thing would be the film. The book had been reviewed on the front page of the *New York Times*, he said. His attitude was, if the film business didn't react they weren't worth the money copiously paid them.

Within a few days two interesting production houses had indeed responded. One was Goldcrest, the British company which had recently made the film *Gandhi*. The other was Amblin, Steven Spielberg's production company at Universal. Apart from Fred Schepisi's *The Chant of Jimmie Blacksmith*, I had had a few other experiences with film companies. Another book of mine, *Gossip from the Forest*, had been painlessly translated by Granada TV in Britain into a film for television. It had been shot in the forest near Chester, and I had been invited to visit the shoot but had never managed to do so.

I was something of a film option skeptic, in fact. Many of my books had been optioned by American, British or Australian producers. There seemed a pattern to the way things flowed. When a producer first approaches a writer, he or she is unapologetically in love with the book. To realize it in film is his sole desire. And the uniqueness of the book will override any of its problems, which he admits there are, but rather like the dimples of the beloved. And so he wants to tie up your book for a year or so by offering a small option price on the understanding that when he gets the money to make it, the horn of plenty will open, there will be a full contract and a glorious payday.

But after the producer has visited a number of studios, other funding sources and production companies, his ardor is always somewhat muted. The book now presents a series of real challenges—perhaps that it's a period piece; that it belongs to a genre to which three other recently failed films belong (bye-bye uniqueness!); that the studios have been stung with projects like this before; that they presented it to the agent of the beloved actor of the moment, but the beloved actor and his agent had "passed on it." The producer with whom you have the modest option deal has been trying intermittently to find other hunks, but the pre-option unconditional love has gone, and there is weariness in the producer's voice, a warning that nothing miraculous and unexpected is likely to happen. So I did not think this production company interest in Schindler would really lead anywhere.

Meanwhile the book was in print again, and Poldek and I had been invited back to New York to appear on the *Today Show* with Jane Pauley. They wanted Poldek so they could talk about what he had been through with Oskar and how he had placed the story in my hands, and so on. We caught a plane to New York, stayed a night in a hotel, and ended up together on the favorite morning TV show of the United States. I had told Poldek at dinner the night before that television is a frantic medium. A ruthless lack of elbow room prevails. One's message has to be scaled down to a degree of rigor such as, I could see with some dread, was not in Poldek's character to achieve.

We were made up by early morning cosmeticians who had

applied pancake to every senator and rock star in America. In the green room in the studio in New York, Poldek was an instant hit with all the other guests, praising gifts of feature and talent in them. When they asked what he was doing there, he pointed to me as his Cervantes and told everyone to watch out for the movie. Poldek similarly tried to make a lifelong friend of the stage manager who ushered us onto the set between commercials. The producer of our segment approached us nervously and told him we would have eight minutes.

"Eight minutes," he said. "That's not nearly enough. You are a fine woman. Could you, darling, get us at least ten?" But the television gods were immovable on this.

As Jane Pauley rose to meet us, Poldek confessed his undying love despite the fact that "you are already married to that nice man the cartoonist" (Garry Trudeau, creator of the *Doonesbury* cartoon strip). There was the faintest panic in Jane Pauley's lovely eyes as she hoped some allied presence out in the darkness of the studio might help her to control this force of nature. The floor manager interrupted Poldek's praise of the Trudeau-Pauley marriage by crying urgently, "Thirty seconds!"

Poldek dropped his voice to an Irish whisper. "You must be so tired, darling, working like this every morning. Take care of yourself, Jane. For God's sake, darling. You are still a young woman!"

Jane Pauley nodded when the stage manager said, "Ten seconds."

As the lights came up on us, Pauley introduced us both and asked me about our first meeting, Poldek's and mine. I explained it briskly, and then Poldek explained it with joyous expansiveness, and there was time for one last question. When did Poldek first see Schindler? Poldek told the story of his and Schindler's first meeting at the Pfefferberg home in Grodzka Street in 1939. And suddenly we were being thanked and ushered out of the lit circle of brief national fame in which Jane Pauley remained.

"We did very well, Thomas," Poldek told me on the way to get his makeup off. "But my God, what was wrong in giving us a little more time?"

I noticed that the young minders who ultimately got us from the green room to the street were quite refreshed by Poldek. They were used to folk who had learned by experience of other interviews to say things with the unnatural crispness the media required. It was a trick which, once you were on to it, took no particular gifts. But they had not encountered anything like Poldek's omnivorous goodwill and lack of television pretense.

In terms of telling the story of the book, however, it seemed a catastrophic interview. So I thought then, anyhow. Now, I'm not so sure. As Poldek said in the taxi, "That should make those sons-of-bitch publishers print more and more copies." Indeed, soon after this interview, the print run of the book, as Poldek had promised, sold out again.

And as we returned to California, November 1982 turned to December.

The message had come through the U.S. publisher that Steven Spielberg, whose *E.T.* was flickering from innumerable cinema screens throughout the world, wanted to see me on the following Saturday at the house of Sid Sheinberg (the head of Universal) in Bel Air.

"I'll go too," Poldek told me when he heard.

"I think I'm the only one invited, Poldek."

"Don't be ridiculous. I know Spielberg's mother. I eat at her restaurant all the time. She's a beautiful woman. A tiny woman but gracious."

Indeed, Spielberg's mother, Leah Adler, ran an eclectic kosher dairy restaurant in Beverly Hills called the Milky Way. To prove the point, Poldek took me there a day or two later, and we ate the best kosher food I'd encountered, much better than the King David's. I can't remember the small-boned Mrs. Adler having any protection at that stage from celebrity hunters, or from enthusiastic screenwriters trying to pass on to her scripts for relaying to her renowned son. Much later in the century, she certainly employed a huge yarmulke'd man, reputed to be a former Israeli paratrooper, to repel such nuisances.

Mrs. Adler was a strong woman, a woman of presence. Though she hung Steven's posters on the walls, she admitted that he had mystified her as a child. She would tell one journalist, "I didn't know he was a genius. Frankly, I didn't know what the hell he was."

Poldek, of course, told her all about our coming meeting with her son, news of which she listened to with an ageless tolerance.

On Saturday morning, Poldek, having cleared it with

Steven's office, turned up at the little hotel, comfortably and miraculously remaining in the heart of Rodeo Drive, where I stayed. It was a bright, early winter morning without sea mist, and the air looked auspicious—not nearly as stained as usual. Some breeze from the mountains had flushed it clean overnight. I very much doubted that Spielberg would want to make a film, but it would be fascinating to meet him. Knowing a little about films, I knew not to be too enthusiastic, and as we ascended into the hills it was Poldek who twitched with certainty.

We passed improbable pavilions of marble, and majestic gates through which we saw curving driveways and swards of green almost too perfect to believe in. Extensive stone walls hemmed in mysteries of wealth. Indeed, the streets here were said to be confusingly pretzel-shaped to prevent intrusions into stars' homes by fans or people with ideas for films. Along one of these thoroughfares we chased the number of Sid Sheinberg's place. When we saw it we pulled up to the tall garden gates and I muttered into a voice box with Poldek egging me on. "Tell him you're here to see Steven!" The gates opened.

A house could not yet be seen. It needed to be driven to, atop the hill beyond a screen of tall shrubs. Dickens had never been able to lay claim to such a mansion; James Joyce and D. H. Lawrence were strangers to such places. This was the Bel Air version of Versailles created out of the minuscule filaments called movies, out of the work of screenwriters, blessed and unblessed, and of authors humble and grand. By the time

Poldek had parked the car behind the house in a spot indicated by a muscular man, half waiter, half bodyguard, I felt a little disoriented. But it was Poldek's policy not to be.

"All right," he boomed to me. "Let's go and meet the wonder *boychickel!*"

Sid Sheinberg appeared almost at once in the door of something like a Bel Air conservatory. He was a genial, slim, bald fellow. Physically, he resembled the sort of Californian of whom people said, "He has a tremendous backhand." Obesity was considered God's own curse in Beverly Hills, and he was lean as salvation. Lunch was set in a pleasant room within, where there was so much glass that one felt oneself to be outside anyhow.

Steven had not yet arrived, and we stood talking about such things as the publication of the book and Poldek's experience of Schindler. "Sure I knew him, Mr. Sheinberg. I was black-marketeering for him before he went into business in 1939!" So we took up from where we left off with Jane Pauley. Barely a glass of water had been drunk when Steven Spielberg appeared, having been brought in from the front of the house. He had a fast-moving, Ohio-cum-Californian accent. We shook hands, and he said the sort of things film people always say about books.

Like a true out-of-his-depth colonial boy, I declared, "An honor to meet you, Mr. Spielberg. This is my friend Poldek Pfefferberg, the man who introduced me to the story."

Spielberg was dressed for the weekend, in sports shirt and slacks and sneakers. Of the four of us, Poldek was the only one wearing a tie. And he had no such reverence as mine in store for Spielberg, who now said hello to him and shook his hand.

Poldek said casually, "Steven, I was talking to your mother the other day, and she says you're doing very well." There was a suspicion in his voice that Mrs. Adler might have been exaggerating, and a sort of implied addendum—*If you'd only studied harder in high school like your cousin Leon, you could have been a chartered accountant too.* Thus, I noticed, did old Jews always put successful younger Jews in their place. Not a bad cultural habit, I suppose, but a tough one.

We sat to our light lunch. No wine was served, of course, wine wasn't really the Californian style, despite the splendid vineyards of the north of the state. Spielberg proved to be particularly interested in exactly what I would have wanted him to be interested in—the ambiguity of Schindler, the balance between opportunism and human compassion, the fact that no one could tell where one ended and the other began. And the fact that Schindler, the unself-reflective hero, had been unable to tell anyone either.

Poldek gave his version, of course, and it was the beginning of a communication between Poldek and Spielberg which would last for fifteen or sixteen years.

We were not far into the lunch before Spielberg told Sid Sheinberg he'd like to use his bathroom. Sheinberg gave directions, and Spielberg was barely out of hearing before dapper Poldek appealed to me, "Grossing two million a day, he has to wear sneakers? I ask you!"

But despite Poldek's perception that Spielberg lacked nattiness, in the conversations we had that day the director showed himself an urbane fellow, soft-spoken but still with urgency in his voice. He proved also an accurate reader of the import of the book. And the truth was, grossing two million a day, he was entitled to wear sneakers. He had no concern for fashion.

The lunch drew to a close without any firm undertakings. Poldek assured Spielberg, "I tell you, Steven, you make this film of humanity man to man, it will win you an Academy Award! Guaranteed! No doubt at all!" I had not dared achieve first names with Spielberg myself, but it seemed to present no challenge for Poldek. And Poldek had no problem naming the unspoken entity, the film. "You'll get an Oscar for Oskar!" In case Steven did not understand, Poldek made a similar case to Sheinberg. Spielberg shook my hand. "Fine book, fine book," he murmured. But that was all. It might have been a farewell.

At the little hotel in Rodeo Drive that December, I also met one of the Goldcrest producers. I had greatly admired *Gandhi*, and was convinced Goldcrest, if they made an offer, would do a subtle job not only on Oskar but on the SS's fresh-faced boys and young men who, between unspeakable acts, sent home to their mothers items of Polish linen bought in the Sukiennice. Hollywood did not have as good a record for creating three-dimensional Nazis.

I went back home for another antipodean Christmas, vigorously celebrated by Judy, who took Christmas as seriously as Dickens. Suppressed excitement, astonishing wrapping paper and ribbon, and presents which genuinely did take one by surprise were all part of her Australian Yule-craft. Though it is often a day of some eighty-five to ninety degrees Fahrenheit with considerable humidity, the Australians celebrate Christmas with a thoroughness which leaves them exhausted and hungover.

In the New Year, a young woman named Kathy Kennedy, executive producer of *E.T.* and before that Steven's secretary, made an occasional call about the progress of plans. The usual parsimonious word *option* was thankfully not mentioned. With Universal behind it, Amblin would either buy the rights or not.

As these events were shaping, I got a call on a Wednesday morning, Sydney time, from Amblin, asking me if I could come that night to Los Angeles and sign a contract with Universal. The idea of a contract at once put paid to my skepticism about films. I told Spielberg I would need to be back in Australia on Sunday to give a lecture. That was fine, he said, I could leave Australia Wednesday night, arrive in Los Angeles Wednesday morning by grace of the dateline, sign the contract, confer with my friends Poldek and Glovin. If I caught the Thursday night plane back to Sydney, I would be home on Saturday morning.

It is twelve hours from Sydney to Los Angeles and the flights were then all overnight. Though I was tired, I did not worry about that. I was on my way to what every writer sometimes secretly dreams of: payday. I knew of writers whose rights had been violated and who had been neglected and underrewarded for their films—Ken Kesey, who claimed to have received a mere $10,000 for what he saw as the violation of his book *One Flew Over the Cuckoo's Nest*. I had asked Anthony Burgess, two years before at that BBC studio in Shepherd's Bush, whether it was true that he had received something like fifty pounds for the film rights to *A Clockwork Orange*. He claimed it was. He had been living in Malta, and for some mysterious reason to do with taxes, a rock group had been buying up film properties for small amounts of money and had bought the rights to his brilliant book.

Kathy Kennedy and Steven Spielberg, however, did not seem to intend any malice toward me.

The necklace of bumpy storms always strung across the Pacific between Sydney and California barely woke me in my ample seat—no one in the American film industry flew at the back of the plane, it seemed, the cramped region in which Poldek and I had made all our research trips. Indeed, I was to learn that first class was actually considered hardship travel by Universal's standards, and that one's own private jet was the only ultimately reasonable way for a mogul to get around.

Even though Australians have plenty of practice in sleeping on long flights, the well-rested still arrive in foreign parts a little dislocated. It is as if the brain is somewhere near Hawaii and has not caught up. There is a tendency to slight blurring of vision, accentuated by the smudged air over Los Angeles. There was a booking for me at the Sheraton in Universal City, and I received the room key in the midst of families departing the hotel for a big day in the theme park of Universal Studios.

My friend Poldek visited me. "They get you to come from Sydney for two days? It means they must want to make the film straightaway." That certainly seemed a reasonable proposition.

Chiefly I was full of a quiet anticipation. It seemed that I would be freed from want for some years, from the anxiety of waiting, an overdraft in place, for publishers to accept a manuscript and pay an advance on royalties; of sweating for a release date, when the payment on publication became due.

There was still a little light-headedness and sense of dislocation on the second day, when I was taken across by car to Universal's legal department, an entire white office block in Universal City. All parties were there, under the chairmanship of a Universal lawyer. There was a prenuptial stillness in the room. I wondered if the lawyer was one of those functionaries who kept films in notional debt so that future earnings were not squandered on such people as writers. But this morning the fellow seemed like a kind uncle. In front of him, Spielberg, Sid Sheinberg, Poldek, Glovin (as Schindler's lawyer) and myself all affixed our signatures to the contract. A sweet part of the deal was that I would write the first screenplay, and so I would not need to leave the Schindler story yet—it had become something of a home, even with its foul pit of nightmares and its chancy rescues.

Glovin signed a contract as associate producer, Poldek one as technical adviser. Sid Sheinberg made some pro forma remarks about the day being a happy one, and Spielberg thanked me for coming so far for so short a time. At that moment he was, I believe, editing the first Indiana Jones movie, and its needs pressed on him. We all said farewell to Spielberg, expecting to see him again soon.

I boarded the Los Angeles–Sydney flight and reencountered my distrait and overstimulated brain in the dark air somewhere east of Tahiti. In Sydney, I was met by my wife and daughters at the airport and we went and had coffee, and the universe seemed an abundant place, with the only serpent in the garden being that unarguable reality that all this fruitfulness was based on the mulch of lives taken or closely threatened in the Second World War.

At everyone's insistence, and in the face of my doubts about being able to handle such a mysterious implement, I now acquired a grossly annoying and inscrutable personal computer. The personal computers of the day, 1983, were large, clunky and erratic. But they had something I had always needed—the cut-and-paste facility. It would help a lot with the writing of the screenplay. With the coming of PCs, Barbara, the woman with the office in Avalon who had previously done my and other local transcription work, acquired a video store, and I began to help her make her modest fortune out of late return fees on films.

Fourteen

In the office by the beach, I began writing the screenplay from the familiar material of the book. Naturally, I knew I would find it hard to combine characters, or to get the tumultuous conglomeration of tales contained in the book down to the compass of the screenplay. I particularly did not want to sacrifice the interesting connections Oskar had with the Abwehr, or such incidents as his journey to Budapest to meet Mr. Springmann and company and tell them of the monstrousness being practiced in the camps. I did not, either, try to introduce any false suspense or melodrama, at least no more than that huge amount that existed in the tale already. The film, I felt, should have that feel of intimate experience. And it must have paradox. If Schindler were turned into a stock hero, an unalloyed saint like Raoul Wallenberg, the particularity of Oskar's experience, and that of his prisoners, would be lost.

Obviously, I did not quite know how much of his full story a character like Schindler should carry with him into a film script. For example, could his motorbike rally-racing stand as a model for his later daring? It was my suspicion that a film audience would accept a greater degree of initially unexplained facets of a character than is normal in a novel. And I didn't need to go into such things as why he was a civilian, and thus had escaped conscription, or why he was married to Emilie, a local farmer's daughter in his hometown. The ambiguity between them could be revealed by events inside the film—the arrival of the wife in Kraków, for example. Was this why film stars were so dazzlingly handsome, or had such presence—so that their beauty could sustain the tension of audiences not knowing who they were until events revealed the answer?

The truth is that I knew, at least at the rational if not the emotional level, that to make a film from a book, I must ruthlessly limit the action of the film, so that it is a river of semi-mysterious derivation with no backwaters or billabongs to delay the traveler. And I had to write so that people under forty would not even ask themselves how this man escaped conscription. Or, if they did, the potent momentum of Oskar's adventures must allay such concerns.

I was not a complete screenplay virgin. I had written the screenplay for a television drama named *Essington*, in honor of an ill-fated attempt to create, on the northern Australian coast in the nineteenth century, an alternative port to Singapore. I had written a few other things which had never been produced. I'd dabbled with plays. But in narrative terms, I was temperamentally a novelist, likely to break out into subplots and sub-narrations even when telling a story in dialogue. I en-joy the technique of the screenplay, the rationed description, the attempt to get a complex subtext into what is quite often sparse dialogue. But it was not necessarily natural to me.

At the end of three months, by mid-1983, when I had edited and reedited the screenplay, it was still two hundred and twenty pages long. I delivered it to Spielberg in Los Angeles. Loyal Poldek thought it was exactly what was needed. He would ever after say, "They should have made your screenplay, Thomas!" But in his office at Amblin, in the Universal lot, Spielberg told me that perhaps I was too close to the material. I should give it one more try. I should pretend I hadn't written the book, and that I had the task of making someone else's work—work in which I felt no proprietary right—viable for the screen. And I should try to get the length down. Two hundred and twenty pages were nearly two and a half hours of film. Look at the films in the video stores, said Spielberg. They were 118 minutes up to about 125 minutes tops—the average endurance of the human bladder.

Though I begged him not to, Poldek kept calling Spielberg's office and telling them, "Just make Thomas's script, Steven, and you will have an Oscar for Oskar." Indeed, I could not see what the basic film narrative problem was with what I had written, but then I suppose the screenwriter never can.

For the next eighteen months, I kept working on the screenplay, and on the beginnings of a new novel. Time evaporated, as ever when one is writing hard. Even so, 1985 rolled in without my finding a satisfactory resolution to the writing of the screenplay other than to reduce it in length. It was now that the writing school at the University of California at Irvine asked me to come as a visitor. Oakley Hall, the founder of the program and of the Squaw Valley Summer School to which the nation's notable young writers and top editors and agents were invited, was having a semester's rest and wanted me to take his place.

I went to this campus among the old orange groves of Orange County, inland from John Wayne's Newport. There were some splendid writers among the students at that time. They included Michael Chabon and Whitney Otto, of whom one heard that they wrote astonishing novels in class. Indeed, the most astounding thing about this program was its capacity, built up by Oakley Hall and MacDonald Harris (Don Heiney), to put the students in contact with agents and publishers. The students seemed very companionable, tended to be in their late twenties and upward, and had in most cases already been toughened by the American workshop process, which I found rather harsh, if not brutal. There were twelve graduate writers chosen from all over the country, one of whom—a very engaging young working-class man from San Jose, James Brown—already had a novel, *Hot Wire*, published, and would produce many more.

The process was like this: we met in a dedicated seminar room named "The Writers' Center," and in consultation with the twelve graduate writers—chosen, in theory, from all around the world, but chiefly from North or Central America—worked out who would present a chapter of his or her novel, or a short story, at each of the weekly sessions. Then, for that first week, the visiting writer gave a lecture on his own experience of writing. In subsequent weeks, each novice would have provided us with his chapter/short story and have gotten twelve written critiques, including mine. On top of that I was meant to sum up the responses. Many of the writers in the workshop had been through this experience as undergraduates as well. As a published writer who had never been to any such class, I was nonetheless considered quite up to scratch for managing this situation.

In between pontifications on the art of the novel, I received from Spielberg my writing instructions concerning the script. Thus was the teacher taught. It was now a little more than two years since the contract had been signed. The urgency which had attended the signing had not seemed to translate itself into the pace of preparing it for production. When I went up I-405, exiting at Santa Monica Boulevard to go toward Beverly Hills to visit the Pfefferbergs, I would encounter a slightly glum Poldek, and a philosophic Misia. Though Amblin kept us well-informed of the progress of *our* film, we learned of Spielberg's current projects generally through friends sending us clippings from *Variety* or other magazines or newspapers. Spielberg was about to make Alice Walker's glorious *The Color Purple* into a film, it was said. In fact he already had it in the can. It was also said that he had acquired J. G. Ballard's extraordinary book *Empire of the Sun*—indeed, what book of J. G. Ballard's is not in its way extraordinary, or marked by reminders of mortality and the amorality it produces in the living?

In Spielberg's eyes, I had not overcome the documentary feel of the book. I was still too attached to incidents which did not contribute to the direct line he wanted the screenplay to follow. Indeed, he had now come up with a formula for the film. There would be an SS man whom the charming Oskar could not "corrupt," and who accumulated accusations against him and tried to destroy him. SS Inspector Javert would pursue Jean Valjean Schindler, who had everyone else enchanted, into the final moments of the war. This was not quite the story as I saw it.

Early in that northern spring of 1985, in the nicest possible way, I was sacked by Spielberg. He said he would try some other writers. I had taken to the meeting an E.T. doll that my daughter Jane wanted signed, and I got him to sign it. I was not aware of any bitterness at all, and there was none on my part. I had ideas for new books and felt, however ill-advisedly, liberated. Steven told me he intended to bring in Kurt Luedtke, who had won an Academy Award for the screenplay of *Out of Africa*.

Luedtke, formerly a journalist, brought to the Schindler story a journalist's skepticism. He wanted to begin before the beginning, with the Schindler research itself. At a meeting with him and Gail Mutrux, a young Universal producer who was put in charge of briefing him, Poldek would say with exasperation, "Of course it's all true, Mr. Luedtke. I saw it with my eyes."

Ultimately, and for whatever reason, Luedtke was also unable to produce a screenplay Spielberg wanted to make. I never found out why, but there were rumors he had felt so overwhelmed by the material that he had been unable to produce even a first draft. In the meantime, every time newspapers or magazines mentioned Spielberg's future projects—and there were generally two or three things on the boil at any one time,

including the first Indiana Jones feature—Schindler went un-
mentioned. "I call him and tell him *this* is his film to make,"
Poldek would inform me regularly and with touching bemusement. "But can I make the boy listen? Has he ears?"

Back in Bob Hawke's Australia after the Irvine stint, I had
begun work on a novel about the very first European play performed in all the immensity of the Australian continent, which
was staged by a group of convicts on June 4, 1789. A friend accused me, in my fascination with convicts and Holocaust victims, of being obsessed with the theme of imprisonment.
There was certainly some justice to that idea. But though I had
many alternative lives to deal with, for Poldek his one mission
was Schindler, and as the film script failed to emerge, he was
the terrier who kept barking as the rest of us got on with our
sundry enthusiasms.

At home, I would receive evening calls—that is, late morning calls in Poldek's terms—from his office in Los Angeles,
during which he would detail his conversations with Amblin,
and the messages he passed on to Steven via a good Jewish girl
named Cathy Niebuhr, and the good Irish American girl Kathy
Kennedy. One call in 1987 was different from the rest. Poldek
and Misia were going to come and visit us in Australia. "I can't
get to see enough of your beautiful girls, and that beautiful
Judy," he declared.

With balloons and flowers, we met them in the early morning at Sydney Airport, as they descended from one of the increasingly numerous flights from Los Angeles. The girls had
made signs welcoming them, a gesture which echoed Poldek's
unconditional affection for us. It was a joyous time, of course,

a bright Sydney winter's chance for reunions with Poldek's fellow welder Edek Korn and his wife Leosia, one of the women who had escaped Auschwitz with Misia. There was a slightly later reunion with the accordionist Leo Rosner, a man after Poldek's heart, and his wife in Melbourne. Poldek drew the interest of the local media and gave exuberant interviews, full of his standard predictions. A headline declared, AN OSCAR FOR OSKAR, SAYS SCHINDLER SURVIVOR. If only Spielberg would get on and make the film.

Prime Minister Bob Hawke had an intense, and many said exceedingly partisan, attitude toward Israel. He invited Poldek and Misia to a Labor Party fund-raising lunch, where they sat at his table. Poldek, of course, cherished his time with the rough-edged but clever and amusing prime minister, and Misia was enchanted with the much-admired but utterly unassuming Hazel Hawke, a woman who was not entirely confident in her role, one felt, perhaps because she was not entirely confident in the solidity of her relationship with her husband.

I remember a day when we had a barbecue for Poldek at the Bilgola Surf Club—the sort of place on the edge of the beach where surf rescue gear was stored, and where the members themselves had leisurely Sunday barbecues. The club possessed a beautiful little fenced garden, right by the sea. Poldek exclaimed how lucky we were to be Australians, and Misia extolled the beauties of Sydney, which she had not quite expected. At least one of my daughters had already stayed with Poldek and Misia in California, but as adolescents they were again overwhelmed by his restless energy, his demands that everyone line up because he intended to "make a picture!" "Misia, darling, stand next to Mrs. Keneally, and Margaret, honey, so beautiful, will you close up to your mother just a tiny bit? You're adorable, darling Jane. Such an adorable Australian girl." My father, who liked such parties, possessed in Poldek's eyes the honor of having fought the Nazis in North Africa.

And still the opening gambits—"I called Steven . . . ," "I tell Steven all the time . . ."—were the staple of Poldek's conversation. Not for effect, either. Though raucous, he was not a boastful man, and offered nothing for effect except his flattery, which itself, by mere force of character, sounded like the truth.

I was privately sure, though, that nothing would happen with the proposed film now. Fred Schepisi, the Australian director whom I was occasionally lucky enough to meet socially, either in Australia or at his apartment in New York, told me that the response to *The Color Purple* and to *Empire of the Sun* had convinced Spielberg that the critics were determined not to give him a fair hearing as a serious producer and director. Yet still, Steven had made some approaches to the renowned playwright Tom Stoppard to work on a Schindler screenplay. Meanwhile, press reports showed he was busy on a huge project named *Hook*, a retelling of Peter Pan, and as far from Schindler as one could get.

Scattering thanks behind them, after a month Poldek and Misia caught the plane home. I could see in both of them an authentic and touching gratitude for the small mercies of food, sunlight, brotherhood.

Fifteen

In the late 1980s to early 1990s, I traveled to Eritrea in the fraught Horn of Africa, took on a visiting professorship at delightful NYU, headed the movement to make Australia a republic, and was offered and accepted a post at the University of California at Irvine, and still the film had not been made.

In the Irvine writers' program, I was not the only one who had an unproduced book with a film studio, and indeed a number of films based on the books of writers who had been graduate students when I was last at UCI were in the process of production. Kathy Kennedy, Spielberg's executive producer, took me to lunch in 1991 to tell me the young man named Steve Zaillian was now working on the Schindler screenplay, and also introduced me to the Australian director Jocelyn Moorhouse, who was slated to make the film of Whitney Otto's *How to Make an American Quilt*, a book written during Otto's participation in the UCI program. Marti Leimbach's novel *Dying*

Young was in production by Joel Schumacher and starred Julia Roberts. The film rights were in the market for Michael Chabon's *Wonder Boys.*

Talking writing was a compulsive exercise with the graduate students. There was not one of them who was not a splendid writer. The only question was: Who would be hungry enough, desperate enough, to write their book, and then write another? It is not an easy business. Enough of them who could write were in for years of heartbreak until their books were at last published, or else they would become teachers in universities and junior colleges. To tell a young writer he had talent when it was not true was my version of the sin against the Holy Spirit, for it condemned them to a severe regime embarked upon without the tools to give it meaning. Indeed, to find out that you did not have literary talent was in some senses the equivalent of being told you did not have hepatitis. It meant your life would not be driven by the characteristic pattern of obsession, exaltation, depression, recurrent disappointment at not being the writer you hoped to be, and all the grief that this would impose on your family.

Poldek and I still met up for occasional meals. He came down, sometimes with Misia, sometimes without, to readings at the university or to brunch at the Laguna Hotel. I would go up occasionally to attend his 1939 Club events. Sometimes we would be invited somewhere—UCLA, UC Santa Barbara, or the Claremont Colleges, say—to do our act, to tell our joint story. And in more modest gatherings, at readings at Barnes & Noble in LA or Orange County or San Diego, I would read from my new books, from *Woman of the Inner Sea*, for example, over which no Amblin aura hung.

We were a good team, and an act in contrasts. I always signed the Schindler book with *Shalom, Peace*—a much dishonored word in any language. He signed his ornately. *A man who saves a single life saves the world entire*. Then, *A story of humanity man to man*. Sometimes he would add, *Always remember not to forget!* Then, *Professor Magister Leopold Pfefferberg*. In a world in which most professional writers are stingy with their signatures, Poldek wrote an essay, and the phenomenon ensured that there were some late nights in bookstores for us. On top of that, since the American edition had halftone prints, he would say, "Look at page forty-nine, darlings, and see what a good-looking Polish officer I was!"

Back to the beach we came each year as summer struck Southern California and fires raged down out of the shrublands behind the ocean. In the kindly Sydney winter of 1991, I was as engaged as ever in writing a novel when the news came, first of all and appropriately from Poldek.

"Thomas, have you been told? At last our friend Steven is going to make the film. We are *there*, my brother!"

"Are you sure, Poldek?"

"Do you think I'd want to lie to a friend?"

"It's just been a long wait, Poldek."

"Ai, ai, ai!" he said, in a lament for the lost time. "But he got the flu, and he read the book again and said, 'It's time. I must make this film.' This guy Steve Zaillian, a nice man, he's the screenwriter. He's doing the final polishings. My friend, I see it all happening now, and the Novell Prize is close, and I have my ticket booked to Stockholm."

"Yes. I know, Poldek. You'll be there on your own."

"It will happen, it will happen! Didn't I tell you the film would be made?"

"You told me. And that finance policeman back in Kraków."

"That guy. I should look him up, the poor guy. But I lost his address."

I got a confirmatory call from the admirable Kathy Kennedy. When I returned to UCI, Steven would want to see me, she said. Zaillian's screenplay was on its way to me, and comment would be welcomed. From Spielberg's secretary came the suggestion that I was entitled, along with all the other writers, to claim a screen title and have the matter adjudicated by the Writers Guild of America. The screenplay, when it arrived, read well, and I was delighted to see some of what I thought of in writer's vanity as the book's more significant phrases and images intact within it. It showed that Steve Zaillian was not too proud to use his chief source. I did not have the bewildering experience of seeing a transformed, skewed and misused tale. There were sections of the Schindler story missing, of course—Schindler's career with the Abwehr, for example, and his childhood. His postwar career was covered in a few lines. That was the inevitability of film. Zaillian had done a splendid job.

Over the next few weeks, the first panel of three experi-

enced members of the Writers Guild of America had convened
to compare the two screenplays, Zaillian's and the equally hefty
document I had written in Australia in the early 1980s. Their
judgment was that Steve Zaillian deserved a sole writer's
credit. I was mildly surprised, since my earlier screenplay had
been as documentary in feel as Zaillian's now was, but I was
satisfied, and did not undertake an appeal, even though Amblin made it obvious that it was no skin off their nose if I did.

Poldek called and asked me what I thought of Zaillian's
script. We both liked it, although he confessed that early on he
had called Spielberg and said, "Steven, I'm just up to page
fifty-five and—*already* thirty mistakes!"

Judy and I returned to UCI for the Southern Californian
winter, and moved into one of the houses up in University
Hills behind the university, built across the old prairie and or-
chard hills of the Irvine ranch. I resumed the workshops and
had begun a new novel, a sort of homage to my immigrant
grandparents, named *A River Town*.

I had also, with the help of the chairman of the English Department, acquired a reader's ticket at the wonderful Huntington Museum up in Pasadena, beneath the San Gabriel Range
and its attractive snowcaps. The Huntington was meant to
complement research I had already been pursuing in the New
South Wales archives and elsewhere on Irish convicts transported to Australia—the world they had been ejected from, the
world they encountered in the convict planet of Australia, and
the world of America to which in some cases they escaped.

It was in the midst of research, teaching and writing that I got a call from the charming Bonnie Curtis, Steven's new assistant at Amblin, asking me to come and see Steven, and apologizing that it would require a schlep up 405 and the aging I-5 freeway to get there.

Turning up in one's car at a studio and being admitted at the gate, the real gate, the gate of business, is itself an archetypal scene in movies, a scene of savage rejection or unlikely triumph. Despite every resistance, every effort to seem normal, casual and a non-stranger, the myth works on you, even though studios generally look like some physically nonpolluting warehouse and manufacturing business. The headquarters of Amblin, however, had never been like that. Near the edge of the Universal set, it was nonetheless the sharp little tail which wagged the big dog of Universal and sent nutriment its way.

In the foyer of Amblin in early 1992 there were exciting artifacts on display in the entryway—the fantastical flying bike from *E.T.*, native American costumes and art, and relics of *Back to the Future.* The place had a marked New Mexican pueblo architectural style, and far more individual grace than the standard offices of other production companies I had visited.

It was now some six years since I had seen Steven in the flesh. I had seen his mother, however, for Poldek had recently taken me back again to Leah Adler's eclectic kosher restaurant; she now had a hefty man in a yarmulke at her side to protect her from molestation by overeager screenwriters and producers.

We met in Steven's relatively modest office and later went on to a lunch of Southwestern cuisine in a dining room. Steven still seemed young, but given his facial hair, one could almost imagine him as a shtetl scholar, telling parables to elucidate the moral and ritual conundra of Torah to a rapt Polish or Russian audience.

He spoke now as if there had never been any doubt he would make this film. "I'm going to make the film someday" had become "I'm now making this film . . ." He said he was ready for it, it was the right time in his life. He had reached an age at which his ancestry and heritage meant more to him than it did when the book first appeared. He had already received Steve Zaillian's script when he caught flu and reread the book, and he said he had then remembered something (he claimed) I had once said to him: "You told me once, 'Just film the bloody book, Steven.' "

I have to say I had no memory of that, or of presuming such familiarity with or influence on him, but maybe I did say it once—bluntness sometimes flows unbidden from Australian lips.

Without detracting from Steve Zaillian's work in any way, since he had written the script in the spirit of the novel, Steven thought following the book was the way to go, even if there would be great lumps of it which he would not be able to find room for. First off, though, he told me he hoped to have Liam Neeson, the Irishman, play the Schindler role. He had considered my genial countryman Jack Thompson (who had acted in *The Chant of Jimmie Blacksmith* as well as many other films), but had decided against him. I had not known this and never got a chance to put in my tuppence-worth on Jack.

In any case, what did I think of Neeson, he asked—purely out of politeness, obviously, since the matter had clearly been decided. I didn't need to pretend. I was fascinated by Neeson's skills as an actor, by the strength of his features. It was a splendid choice, I thought, and it seemed to have been settled. As the "biographer" of the film, Franciszek Palowski, tells us in his book on the ultimate production (*The Making of* Schindler's List), Spielberg had not wanted someone stricken with stardom to do the role. There was a rumor that Kevin Costner had offered to play the part for free. But Neeson had done a screen test, and so had some Polish actors—Piotr Franczewski and Andrzej Seweryn. The latter would end up playing the sinister SS man Scherner in the film.

A little earlier in 1992, said Spielberg, he, his wife Kate, and Kate's mother went to the theater in New York to see Liam Neeson in Eugene O'Neill's *Anna Christie* at the Criterion Center Stage Right, a production in which Neeson played Mat Burke and Natasha Richardson, ultimately to be Neeson's wife, acted Anna. Liam Neeson is said to have been so delighted to see them in the dressing room that he embraced Kate's mother and kissed her on both cheeks with a spontaneity and exuberance which convinced Spielberg that the tall Irishman could do the job. Liam had a growl in his voice, as did Schindler, and he had been practicing off a tape of a filmed speech given by Oskar at Temple Beth Am in Beverly Hills.

And what of Ben Kingsley as Stern? Kingsley brought subtlety to playing decent men, I thought. Superb. Indeed, since *Gandhi* I had felt affronted whenever producers decided to use him as a villain. There was something in his performances as villains which lacked dimension, and in such a fine actor this could only be the fault of writers, directors and casting agents.

Then Steven began to tell me how he meant to film it. In a more documentary style, and with a feel of authenticity, and so in black and white, he said, like the old newsreels from the war, with just a few points of color a few times in the film. Perhaps it was only the candle flame at the start of the film which would be colored, and all else grainy white and black and shades of dun.

I nodded. Secretly, I thought it was a crazy idea. For one thing, to the people *in* the newsreel, what was happening involved far too vivid and brutal color. Later I heard the rumor that highly placed people in Universal were uneasy too, except that Steven had the authority, on the basis of how often he had made them look good, to film it the way he chose.

Steven said he intended to send his producer Branko Lustig, who himself was a childhood Auschwitz survivor, looking for an appropriate city. From what I'd seen of Kraków, asked Spielberg, could it be filmed there?

I told him that as far as I knew, all the sites were still intact—he could film some of Schindler's factory scenes in Schindler's factory, if he could get permission. Kraków's old churches, and the old Jewish sector of Kazimierz and the Nazi ghetto, were intact. So was the site of Płaszów, retained as a national monument and left largely bare because of the evil that was done to Poles—Jews and Gentiles—there. I made the point, too, that the acid rain from the Soviet-built steelworks at Nowa Huta produced a sinister grime upon the gargoyles and the cornices of Kraków, giving an impression of tainted elegance and lost innocence.

We started to talk about Schindler's motivation then, his

mixed motives for employing Jews, his desire to be seriously rich, and all the rest of it. But then he achieved in Brinnlitz something that the good, respectable executives of many leading German companies, including Krupps, IG Farben and Mercedes-Benz, could not manage. He kept his people alive. I mentioned and attempted to reprise Schindler's statement of expenditure, the one to do with the running of the two camps as benign institutions. That was the document, mentioned earlier, which Schindler submitted to the Joint Distribution Committee when impoverished in the late 1950s. I spoke of the way Schindler kept Brinnlitz going as an armaments camp when in fact it ran purely as a black-market base, Oskar having expressed to a number of his Jewish intimates that he did not intend to make anything which would take "some poor bastard's life."

In lunchtime conversation we revisited the issue of where in Oskar altruism ended and opportunism began. I made the claim that it was actually important that the question could not be answered, that the abiding attraction of Schindler's character was wrapped up in the very conundrum.

Last of all, I asked Steven if he could possibly reverse my mistake of years before and name the film *Schindler's Ark*. He said he would do it except that he wanted to use lists throughout. Lists were visible, metaphors weren't. From start to finish it would be a matter of lists. I thought his reasons much better than Dan Green's all those years before. All at once it was midafternoon, and Steven made an arrangement for one further meeting.

In the event, Steven himself would make an initial thirty-

six-hour raid on Kraków in late winter–early spring of 1992.
Spielberg, his assistant Bonnie Curtis, and his trusted, experienced and eternally calm coproducer Jerry Molen, along with
the writer Steve Zaillian, met with the Polish film authorities
in Kraków, especially with Lew Rywin, the head of Heritage
Films, who would work with Steven as a coproducer. They visited all the places associated with the tale, including an excursion into the Nazi-established ghetto from the hill beyond it.
Spielberg made a record of everything with an eight-
millimeter video camera.

Then they raced out to Auschwitz. Concerned by the way the
modern city was impinging upon camera angles at Płaszów,
Spielberg decided to film the camp in the nearby Liban chalk
quarry, a moonscape hole, notably atmospheric and stark on
the black-and-white film Spielberg ultimately shot. The visit
seems to have greatly stimulated Steven. Poldek's friend Franciszek Palowski, who was part of the Polish group working with
the production team, called up Poldek and related how Spielberg had told a Polish television crew that in Kraków he would
make his "truest" film.

Branko Lustig, a bearish, efficient fellow, spent longer pe-
riods in Poland, and although there was some delay over demands that Polish extras be heavily insured, it was ultimately
decided the film would go ahead there early the next year. That
had pretty much become the plan by the time Judy and I went
home to Australia in the North American spring, our autumn. I
was kept informed of further developments by Amblin and by
an exhilarated and hopeful Poldek.

But not everyone would be as tickled as Poldek to see Oskar's name become a byword of "humanity man to man." Poldek intimated to me he had lost some friends when the book was published—chiefly because people were afraid Oskar's story would give the Nazis absolution for their crimes. And Emilie's Argentinian minders had no affection for wife-abandoning Oskar either.

It was about June 1992 that Spielberg went again to Poland and spent a little longer in Kraków. The Hotel Cracovia, one of Oskar's joy spots, was looked over, and a jazz café named Michael's Cave in the Rynek. And places less associated with pleasure—the Pomorska and Montelupich prisons. On this June trip Spielberg stayed at the Hotel Forum near an old tannery building which he wanted to check out as a possible location for Schindler's factory in Brinnlitz. It was a mere two minutes' walk from the Hotel Forum, where Spielberg intended to house his cast and crew. As for the Płaszów camp, Spielberg told Lew Rywin to build a replica of it in the Liban quarry he had just revisited. The production designer who would ultimately do the job was Allan Starski, an expert in designing concentration camps, since he had been the designer for *Europa Europa* and *Escape from Sobibor*.

I still did not quite believe it would all happen. Poldek, however, was exultant. Though there was a rumor that others at Universal considered Steven's intention to make the film a folly, Poldek saw it as plain sense.

Leopold (Poldek) Pfefferberg in Kraków in March 1939, age twenty-six.

Poldek in his uniform as First Lieutenant in the Polish Army, November 1938.

Tom with Ben Kingsley. In the back left of the picture is Jonathan Sagall, who played the young Poldek, showing an uncanny likeness to the original subject.

A much older Poldek pictured with Tom during their research trip to Poland in 1981, a year after their first fateful meeting in Poldek's store in Beverly Hills, California.

Oskar Schindler in equestrian garb, ready to take a ride through the parklands of Kraków in June 1942. It was on one such excursion with his mistress that he was said to have witnessed one of the first and fiercest ghetto raids to round up those Jews seen to be unproductive, for the purpose of systematic extermination.

Schindler (top left) enjoying a German party in Kraków, circa 1940–41.

Schindler (left) with an Abwehr officer, said to be Lieutenant Martin Plathe, with whom Oskar collaborated against the rival SS officers.

Schindler charming friends and clients at a party in Kraków.

Historic photos of women hauling trolleys containing quarried stone at Płaszów concentration camp. These photos, with a number of others, were taken by the Austrian Raimund Titsch, a brave factory supervisor.

A Titsch picture of German and Ukranian soldiers marching through Płaszów concentration camp.

The camp was rather chillingly re-created for the film *Schindler's List* on the site of the nearby quarry, where, during the Holocaust, Jewish prisoners from Płaszów were put to work.

The all-too-real Płaszów camp commandant, Amon Goeth, on the balcony of his residence overlooking the camp. From here he would fire random shots at prisoners with his sniper rifle.

Amon Goeth, a nightmare figure to prisoners, fully uniformed and mounted.

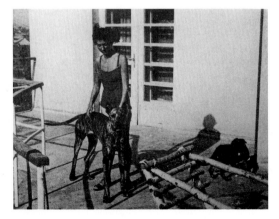

Majola, Goeth's mistress, on the balcony of his residence at Płaszów

Historic photos like those on the facing page allowed Spielberg and actor Ralph Fiennes to re-create with some authenticity the brutal character of Goeth. Spielberg spoke to Tom of how Fiennes, in his uniform as Goeth, was embarrassed when one of the Jewish women survivors visiting the set had backed away from him on trembling legs.

The film reenactment of the scene in which Goeth's house-and-stable boy, Lisiek, is shot dead by his master's sniper rifle for supposedly mishandling a saddle.

Ralph Fiennes as Amon Goeth.

Goeth's residence as re-created for the film *Schindler's List*.

A still from the film of Jews at a checkpoint during an *Aktion* in the ghetto in Kraków. Those with work permits were allowed to work at Oskar's and other factories, while many others—children, the aged and those without labor documents—were gassed in carbon monoxide chambers at the Belzec camp.

The scene in the film in which the Schindler women are mistakenly taken to Auschwitz. They are later rescued as a result of Schindler's intervention and taken to Brinnlitz to work at his factory.

From the film, the women arriving at Schindler's factory after their Auschwitz ordeal.

The famous speech made by Schindler (Liam Neeson) in front of his Jewish factory workers and the SS garrison on the eve of Allied liberation, appealing to the German soldiers to ignore orders to exterminate all prisoners.

Schindler (Neeson) breaks down as he bids farewell to his factory workers, distraught that he was not able to save more Jews. In reality his camp was already crowded beyond its authorized limits.

Tom in front of Spielberg's specially built set of the Płaszów concentration camp. Tom is standing on a re-creation of the path made from the gravestone fragments taken in the war from the nearby Jerozolimska Synagogue, and used by the Germans to pave the entrance to the camp.

Tom in 1993 at 4 Lipowa Street, where Schindler had his office, works and, ultimately, the barracks of DEF, Deutsche Email Fabrik (German Enamel Company) in Kraków.

Tom and his daughter Jane at the monument of Chujowa Górka (Prick Hill), originally the site of an ancient Austro-Hungarian hill fort used by the SS as a screened enclosure in which to slaughter and bury Jews, partisans and people living on forged documents. As the Russians approached Kraków, the bodies were dug up by the SS and burned in a hor-rifying attempt to destroy the evidence of their atrocities.

Officers of the Kraków fire department making "snow" outside a local parish church. It was for a scene (not used in the film) in which Schindler asks a priest to sell him church ground for the Goleszów cattle-truck people to be buried as Jews.

Sixteen

Whenever we left for the United States, I was aware that my father's health was declining, even though he was only in his mid-eighties and thus considered himself young. He profoundly disbelieved in the medical process, and so all medical and hospital ritual was an agony to him. He had got the idea, perhaps from his Irish parents, that whiskey toddies for congestive illness, and methylated spirits and friar's balsam applied to abrasions or wounds, were God's own pharmacy and sovereign cures. Despite hip problems he was robust and drank his whiskey in the evenings, commenting with a vigorous gift for language on politics, world and Australian. He was beloved by all his grandchildren, for whom his interest, his willingness to encourage, and his tendency to sing profane World War II ditties were limitless.

There were no signs of imminent trouble for him, however, when we returned to UCI in September. In the previous Californian winter we had often visited Death Valley, when there would be snow on Dante's View and dry, temperate air down in the valley's big sump below sea level. We would drive out there on Friday evening, and return on Sunday night. I had to take work with me, because I was that sort of obsessive fellow, and in any case my graduate workshop was normally on Mondays. But what always astounded us was that at Bad Water Basin, one looked up from 282 feet below sea level to snowy Telescope Peak, 11,000 feet up in the Panamint Mountains to the west.

One Sunday morning we were out at Death Valley when we got a call from Australia. It was my brother's opinion, one which as a doctor he was competent to make, that my father was dying in the Repatriation Hospital, the hospital for war veterans, and I should come home. I would need to catch that all-too-familiar plane that night from Los Angeles to Sydney. Looking at the map, I attempted to drive out of Death Valley via the shortest route—Emigrant Canyon Road—and to our amazement, in the pleasant hills just beyond Stovepipe Wells and its dunes, we were stopped by snow, and had to retrace our way back to the more accustomed north-south route, the California 374.

The threat to my father's life passed—he recovered as he always seemed to. There was a promise of his immortality in the way he recovered from illness, and in the racy lines he fed us as he was recuperating. In the Repatriation Hospital the morning after I got back, I was delighted to hear him swear at the trouble he was having trying to connect with a bedpan.

"Get in there, you little bastard," he urged. It was a symptom of survival that he began to speak in profane terms again. I commiserated with him from beyond the curtain. "Oh," he said, "the useless bloody thing's like a baby concertina!"

One tale he had told me about the war was of the time he and a dozen or so other men were traveling somewhere in the Indian Ocean on a Norwegian freighter. The Japanese had just entered the war, and at night he and the others would sleep on the deck in life preservers outside the radio shack, listening to distress calls coming in from nearby ships being downed by Japanese submarines and, under orders of radio silence, being unable to answer, and waiting to be torpedoed themselves. The torpedo did not come. The child in me thought they would never make the bullet that could get my father.

Steven was about to make *Jurassic Park*, even in the teeth of Poldek's disapproval. "Stop playing around with dinosaurs, Steven. I promise you, you'll get an Oscar for Oskar." At a further meeting before heading off to film his dinosaurs, Steven had let me know that the English actor Ralph Fiennes had been bulking up for the role of sensual, brutal Amon Goeth. At first sight, Fiennes seemed better suited to playing, say, the tragic young poet Rupert Brooke in a British film about World War I, but Spielberg had seen the possibility of coldness and menace in those gentle eyes. Steven also very warmly invited me to visit the set whenever I could. To just let Amblin know.

To a director, having the writer of the original work on a film set is rather like having a mother-in-law on the honeymoon. I feared that I would be a bit of a spare tire in Kraków, but there was a powerful attraction to the invitation. I began to clear a space between my obligations to UCI. As for Poldek, he was going too, as the hub of the crowd of survivors whom Spielberg welcomed to the set, or whom he would film at Schindler's grave in Jerusalem. Secretly, Poldek did not feel well, and it was something to do with his heart again. He would need to go to the hospital soon, but he kept it pretty quiet. He still had a fair amount of stress from his business, too. "I'm still in a two-way squeeze," he told me once, because the big chains in the nearby Beverly Center made the small dealers he supplied close down, often owing him money. By the late 1980s, he had made a decision to close down the Handbag Studio. His genial son, Freddy, stuck by him in the warehouse side of the business, and though Poldek still showed energetic concern for the Schindler project, at one meeting he cried, "The business is not what it was. People don't pay what they owe like they did when I first came out here."

Personal finances are like people's personal health, crucial and tragic to the sufferer but tedious to the listener. In Australia, many thought I was a radical for my republican stance. In fact there was as much petit bourgeois in me as in any lucky working-class boy. I thought it was time to secure my own old age, but due to normal mug-punter's unwise attempts at investment, I was not traveling too well financially myself. The film did not seem to offer any certain deliverance from that, since some thought of it as Spielberg's folly. I was relieved, therefore, to hear from my American agent, Amanda Urban, that International Creative Management, the company in which she was something of a fabled literary agent, had a lecture department.

The agent who managed lectures for a number of writers and quasi-writers, including General Schwarzkopf, hero of the Gulf War, was Carol Bruckner, who liked to say she was as "Jewish as Paddy's pigs." She was a splendid woman, somewhere between thirty-five and forty-five, with a rich New York sense of humor, along with suspicions of the way Zionism had gone at the end of the twentieth century. I would find that she looked after her lecturers like a mother. Every possible convenience and comfort was placed in their way, so if there was a doubt about what awaited them, she simply canceled. She did not have to cancel often, because those she dealt with knew what she expected for her boys and girls.

It was the lecture circuit, after-dinner and occasional speaking all over the United States, from Detroit to Louisiana, which would in the end pay off all my debts. I would simply talk. Poldek was often the hero of the lecture. When the inevitable query arose during question time—"Have you met Steven Spielberg?"—I was able to tell with mock grief the tale of my dismissal as screenwriter.

I delighted in and enjoyed it, and with Carol Bruckner in charge, I did not face too many unexpected ambushes or demands. At a well-known liberal arts college in the Midwest, Poldek and I did our old double-act to a basketball stadium full of people, and we signed copies of the Schindler book until two a.m., Poldek inscribing every book with his extensive legend about *humanity man to man*, and still signing himself *Professor Magister Leopold Pfefferberg*.

The year 1992 ended without any huge sense of anticipation that the film would grasp the world's attention. Poldek was the only man of certainty in all this. When he went on predicting the Academy Award, everyone indulged him and chuckled. Steven had been editing *Jurassic Park*, and its release was the sensation Universal wanted it to be. By contrast, the marketing budget for *Schindler* was minuscule.

After the release of *Schindler's List*, ill-informed or anti-Semitic people would opine that this was exactly the sort of film you'd expect from Hollywood. After all, the Jews out there pushed the idea of the Holocaust against all the evidence of such scholars as David Irving! So naturally they'd make a movie like this! If that were so, they were very, very slow to do so, and intended to be very wary in promoting it. Poldek asked our old friend Sid Sheinberg, with whom he had been in regular contact since our lunch ten years past, about its release. "We'll have to see about that, Poldek," said Sid. Poldek told me, "Thomas, they're not getting ready at all." Misia, more composed, declared, "Poldek thinks people are going to want to see this story as if it were a big adventure with dinosaurs. He can't understand that people might not want to see what happened to us."

By Christmas 1992, my father's health had got much better. The Australian summer helped. He sat on the balcony of his flat and soaked up the sun. In California, I had almost finished the novel about my grandparents in their general store in northern New South Wales. But first, *Woman of the Inner Sea* came out, a book of mine based on a tale I'd heard some years earlier from an American woman, about the loss of her children, but set in Sydney and the Australian bush. I was doing a series of interviews, and Malachy McCourt, the ultimately famous Frank McCourt's brother, visited us briefly in Orange County with the Irish film director Jim Sheridan. We kept some sedate Orange County waiters up late one night with a medley of disreputable Irish and Australian songs. Malachy told me that if *Woman* was ever to be made into a film, he wanted to play the not-so-Reverend Frank, the heroine's starting-price bookmaker and priest-uncle. *Woman of the Inner Sea* looked to me a pretty long chance as a film. But weren't they all?

Seventeen

According to Franciszek Palowski, Spielberg arrived in Poland
to initiate the project on the morning of February 24, 1993,
and had rented a house in the Wola Justowska suburb of
Kraków which contained an editing suite where he could continue to work on *Jurassic Park*. Steve Zaillian was with him and
was put to work on copious rewrites provoked by the authenticity of the film locations and other factors.

The first scene was to be of ghetto inhabitants shoveling
snow on Poselska Street. Tons of snow had been ordered from
various locations, including mountainous Zakopane, but it
turned out that it was not needed, for overnight on March 1,
1993, the first day of filming, snow had been plenteously
dumped from the sky and the air was full of ice crystals. The
designer, Allan Starski, had merely to cover a modern awning
of a grocery store and add a few period signs to make the scene
work. Thus Scene 75 was shot, the hardy Polish extras bravely
shoveling snow with their bare hands until Spielberg called,

"Cut!" at 8:30 a.m. Then cameras, crew and actors moved to the ancient ghetto of Kazimierz and spent the afternoon filming ghetto scenes.

Lew Rywin, the Polish producer, was wary of the lack of success films on the Holocaust had previously had. He also feared that the cost would be driven up because everyone in Poland who cooperated with Spielberg would expect huge payments. Branko Lustig, the hearty and highly efficient Slav who had executive-produced and coproduced so many renowned films, and Spielberg's habitual producer Jerry Molen—Utah-born, a Mormon, and a man of exceptional generosity of soul—were good at damping down this expectation.

Poldek himself was in hospital in LA at this time. Routine stuff, he told us. A stent or shunt had been inserted in one of his heart vessels. But he was back working by the day filming started. His early return to the office seemed to support the idea that the procedure was minor. But his heart problems were not simple matters, as it turned out.

In Australia again, Judy and I received an invitation to be observers at Eritrea's independence-from-Ethiopia referendum. Judy was just as anxious as I was to attend this great fete of Eritrean survival, whereas she considered herself too busy to go on to the set in Kraków—unlike the rest of the world, she did not much admire film people. My daughter Jane, an economics graduate from the University of New South Wales who wished to become a producer, was willing to come along.

Jane is a smallish, handsome woman, very voluble like her father, but far ahead of me in her gifts of organization. As a result, of course, Poldek and she had always got on extremely well. She could bedazzle and confuse officials nearly as well as Poldek.

I did not go straight to Poland from that East African electoral festival. I had a night's buffer in Rome between the exaltation of referendum Eritrea and Kraków. Exhausted, I fought the normal impulse to wake myself up with liquor, and envied those fortunate souls upon whom whiskey and gin had a soporific, not an arousing, effect.

Kraków airport had changed, I saw upon landing from Rome, since the night Poldek had snowed the Polish official over our exchange documents. There were no Kalashnikovs in sight anymore. Advertising for fruit juices or the unavoidable Coca-Cola filled the airport with their ersatz glitter. *Ski Zakopane!* I was exhorted. The sort of dread and anxiety my financial imbalance had imbued in me seemed to belong to a planet far removed from this sunny Polish afternoon.

By the Planty, the green verges on the south bank of the Vistula, a new Hotel Forum rose and was largely occupied by the actors and crew of the Schindler movie. I was driven to it in a Mercedes by a Pole named Jerzy who told me that he was my driver for the extent of my visit. After he had dropped me at the hotel, he said, he would be going out to the airport again to meet my daughter Jane's flight from America.

By now Steven had overcome a number of challenges to his intentions. Preparing to film the five scenes set in Auschwitz-

Birkenau, Spielberg had got an initial approval from the World Jewish Congress. But one of its vice presidents fought the proposal, and a story broke as early as mid-January 1993 that they were now trying to prevent Spielberg's filming inside the camp. Branko Lustig, who had been a prisoner in Auschwitz, felt deeply offended at having his and Steven's intentions questioned, but now the International Council of the State Museum in Auschwitz joined the World Jewish Congress in opposition. Although Spielberg went to New York to argue his case in a meeting with both these bodies, and to work out the strict criteria for his filming, in the end he decided it was better not to film inside Auschwitz itself but more or less on its doorstep; to build replicas of huts *outside* the gates of Auschwitz, and to have only the trains placed inside, so that when these steamed out through Auschwitz-Birkenau's famous gates the camera would be placed to catch them. For the filming at Auschwitz, the weather had been ferociously cold and snowy, and all this added to the desperation of extras, guards and actors playing prisoners.

In these early days, Steve Zaillian was frequently working late, attending to the expansion and revision of his screenplay. By the time of my arrival, Spielberg had filmed some of Schindler's office scenes in the building that had once been DEF/Emalia, and which the Telpod corporation now occupied. Telpod was having business difficulties at the time, and the company was probably happy to let Spielberg use the premises for a fee.

Poldek had been at the set the week before. He had by now

turned eighty—his birthday was celebrated the week before he packed to go to Kraków. On arrival in his home city, he had left his luggage at the hotel to come straight on to Kazimierz, which was serving as the Nazi ghetto for the film. He and Misia had a Polish painting they had brought to give to Steven, a sort of midway good luck token. There is a picture of Poldek, as dapper as when we walked these streets together in 1981, his arm through Ralph Fiennes's, shoulder to shoulder with Ben Kingsley, as everyone gets ready to shoot the liquidation of the ghetto. Poldek is looking around with a faint frown of incredulity on his face, at the masses of extras, the reincarnations of prisoners and SS guards. He made this happen, but now he seems a little astounded. His hair still has color, and if some of it derived from a bottle, then that is, I know, merely part of the duty of being well-groomed. He does not look an old man. He looks as young as when I first met him. From the animation of his face, one would judge him a fellow upon whom death has no designs.

Thirty thousand extras were used for this scene of the ghetto liquidation, and for production purposes many TV antennae had to be removed from roofs. Poldek must have been gradually overwhelmed by immediacy and by memory. But this did not show at all when he met the Israeli actor Jonathan Sagalle, slated to play him in the film. "Jonathan, I love you. You're a good-looking guy, but you're nowhere near as good-looking as I was at your age." He would be embarrassed, however, when the film, for the sake of artistic license, showed Poldek black-marketeering inside the great Church of the Virgin Mary in the market square of Kraków. He assured a number of his Gentile friends, including myself, Judy, Kathy Kennedy and Jerry Molen, "You know, I would never black-marketeer in that beautiful church."

During filming on the first day that Poldek was on the set, the small four-year-old Polish girl Oliwia Dabrowska had the task of playing Genia, the little girl in the red coat. She walked with brave purposefulness along the streets, while extras all about reacted to Steven's orders to create a melee of panic and savagery. Steven had once mentioned at a meeting that he intended her to be one of the few patches of color in the film. I never got the chance to ask him why he wanted this vivid dot at the film's center, but I presumed he saw it in terms of a shift to a greater intensity in Oskar's motivation, for the film would have Oskar witnessing this scene from a hill outside the ghetto. I presumed also that Steven wished to honor all the hopeful yet slaughtered children who had perished in the sundry ethnic hysterias of the twentieth, bloodiest of centuries.

The director of photography was a pleasant and talented Pole, Janusz Kaminski, and in filming such scenes he used a conventionally fixed camera together with a handheld camera, since Spielberg wanted cinema verité. Much later, he would famously use the same method in the opening sequences of *Saving Private Ryan*.

Misia, who had been resting and gathering her courage, came with Poldek to the next day's filming. Arriving on the set, she was introduced by Steven to the young Israeli actress Adi

Nitzan, who would play her part, and exclaimed, "You are so beautiful." Poldek cried, "But, Misia, you also are very beautiful. Would I give up all those students who were in love with me for a plain woman?"

The filming that morning was on the hill named Bednarskiego where Schindler, out riding in 1942, observed a Nazi *Aktion* in the ghetto. During a pause in filming Poldek took the trouble to point out to Steven the roof of the Kościuszko Gymnasium, the high school where he had been a glamorous young teacher. He and Misia had been billeted in the ghetto at 2 Jósefinska Street, and Poldek pointed that out also.

After some hours of repetitive technical tests with film, Misia and Poldek had to flee the penetrating, damp cold of the hill above the ghetto where Liam Neeson and the Italian actress Béatrice Macola, both splendid on horseback, both suffused with the glow of good living, looked down amazed on the savagery in the ghetto.

By the time I got to Poland and settled into the Hotel Forum, Poldek had left—he would be meeting up with Spielberg in Jerusalem at a later time, when it was intended that the survivors should place grieving stones on Oskar's grave. The hotel seemed quiet until the cast and crew began to turn up at the end of the day's filming. I expected to be meeting strangers, but Bonnie Curtis, Steven's urbane assistant whom I'd met many times before, arrived at my door and welcomed me, telling me that—after a shower—people met up in the bar downstairs, if I wanted to join them. She also showed me an editing suite at the end of the floor I was on, where some sort of initial editing was done every night—there seemed to be editing suites all over Kraków that Steven used, and I did not quite understand where each of them fitted into the process. Later that night, said Bonnie, there would be a screening of the dailies—the edited takes that had been shot the day before.

Down in the bar, the film people were distinguishable from the Mittel-European businessmen by their manner and high quotient of handsomeness or presence. I sat at a long table at which there were Polish, British and American actors and technicians. Bonnie pointed out young Ralph Fiennes, sitting on his own at the bar. She suggested I should maybe go and sign a book of mine he had been hanging on to and ask him to join our table. She told me that his performance as Amon Goeth was so overpowering that even when he changed out of his SS uniform and let his remarkable eyes unclench, people were a little timid to approach him.

I went up and tentatively introduced myself. I found that nobody could be more reticent than Fiennes, with his lost-child aura. He was a quietly whimsical Hiberno-Englishman, with passions for various writers and for rugby. The strange and enchanting way his smile broke over his face is well known to the world by now, and everything Poldek had said to the men and women of the world about bone structure applied in his case. He produced the book, a travel book I had written on the Southwest of the United States, an area for which I had a great passion. It had once been roundly condemned by the *New York Times Book Review*. Because people all around me pronounced *Ralph* in the English way—*Rafe*, a usage which would become famous when he did—I misheard it as *Ray*, and wrote the inscription as such, and he made no complaint. Later I went and apologized frankly for my gaucherie.

When my daughter Jane arrived from Frankfurt a little later in the evening, she was as confident and full of chatter as ever, much more suited to the scene than her father. We went down to the basement with Bonnie to watch the dailies. Even Liam Neeson himself came into the viewing room with Natasha Richardson. He carried a bottle of red wine and two glasses. There were few other viewers. The lights went out. It can't have been a warm day, the one on which the scene on screen was filmed, but as shot it seemed boiling—there was considerable heat haze implied in the way the film was exposed. We were on a railway siding where a train stood loaded with the result of a gleaning of Płaszów's people. Hands reached out through the gratings of the stationary cattle trucks, and Schindler, in a white suit, arrived and exchanged pleasantries with the lineup of SS men, who were complaining of the heat and waiting for the locomotive to haul the trucks away. Oskar suggested that the trucks be hosed down, a concept which amused Goeth, John and Hujar, the SS men. Since the camp hoses did not reach many of the trucks, Oskar offered to bring some from his own factory. Then followed many takes of water streaming through the grates of the cattle trucks under shirt-sleeved Oskar's instructions. And again, such is the lighting of the scene that one feels in one's own cortex the relief from heat and thirst, even while Goeth wondered why Oskar bothered, given that the people in the trucks were going to die.

In fact, black-and-white film made scenes either hotter or, if the director chose, colder, by way of those grainy polarities of color. During later setups Spielberg talked about what I had seen of the dailies, and I acknowledged that, after seeing a few takes on the screen, I felt that black and white was an inspired idea.

Later, Bonnie introduced me to Liam Neeson and Natasha Richardson. Neeson always liked to send up my Australian accent a bit, then and afterward, addressing me as "cobber" and asking did I need any "tucker" (food), and so forth. I made the point to him that had some nineteenth-century landlord decided to forgive Neeson's ancestors their rent and ship the family to Australia—a not uncommon Irish landlord expedient—he would probably now be a Queensland "walloper" (a cop). Though he was good company, he was no wild man, but restrained and mannerly. The important thing was that on camera he *looked* like a wild man. He gave on film that same impression which reportedly Oskar gave his prisoners—of control being held by the merest margin—and a sense of danger that his exuberance would end by killing them all.

Next morning, my indefatigable daughter knocked on my door. The driver, Jerzy, was waiting to take us to the set. It proved to be a disused freight platform and warehouse, by which was parked a splendid vintage locomotive with, of course, a line of cattle trucks behind it. Spielberg turned up in a vigorous mood and impressed upon us that everything had gone very well. "When we've needed snow," he told Jane and myself, "we've got it. When we've needed sun, we've had it." He

stopped short of implying divine intervention, but others—
Branko Lustig, Jerry Molen—told us the same story with the
amazement of men who are used to things going wrong in
films.

Spielberg spoke of how Ralph Fiennes, in his uniform as
Amon Goeth, was embarrassed when one of the visiting
women survivors backed away from him on trembling legs. He
could switch off the normal, genial, even whimsical light of his
eyes, which would come to characterize him in other films
such as *Quiz Show*, and only a lethal blue blankness would
show.

At Steven's suggestion we looked in on the warehouse where
an extraordinary array of period artifacts had been brilliantly
assembled by Allan Starski and his staff. There were profligate
pyramids of suitcases, piles of shoes, jewelry and silver plates,
and family photos that catalogued the vanished Galician Jewish life—the picnics on the Kościuszko mound, the visits to the
country, the girls on wide skis at Zakopane, grinning and
falling. Similarly, we saw heaps of period clothing, toys and
mounds of spectacles. As we looked, Ben Kingsley came up
and introduced himself. He was an enthusiast for his craft, a
man courtly and polite, who at the end of a scene or a day's
filming often uttered some contextualizing dictum which people remembered, and which they took back to town with
them—a slogan for the enterprise. I would find out that one
evening a drunken businessman at the Forum had approached
one of the Jewish actors and told him it was a pity Hitler hadn't
got him. Kingsley had stepped in upon the angry scene and
quietened the ranting with a classy display of threat, strength

and insistence. He was a tough guy under all his Itzhak Stern diffidence.

As Kingsley spoke with us, thousands of extras turned up on the station platform, playing Jewish deportees. They were told to label their bags, so that their possessions could be sent on. They boarded the cattle trucks, helping each other, and the train moved out. This took some time to film, and then in the post-locomotive silence, the camera (and we) entered the warehouse. We saw men industriously at work in silence, sorting goods under the supervision of an SS man, separating and piling up silverware, jewelry and clothing, as the bags from outside were toted in to be themselves emptied and sorted. These scenes involved a number of takes, but what was wanted out of all these painfully assembled relics was deftly shot, since Spielberg knew how to edit what could have been a repetitive clutter.

I noticed that Spielberg had on his monitor, connected as it was to show the shots on Janusz Kaminski's camera, not only the pages of the script, but the pages of the book as well. I asked myself whether he had done that as a courtesy, but it hardly seemed that among all this creative activity he would have had time to go to that trouble. Later I would find out from Franciszek Palowski's book that it was always the case—Steve Zaillian's pages and the pages of the book were always clipped side by side at the base of the monitor. Naturally I was delighted to see the pages there, sundry lines marked up with colored felt-tipped pens. It gave his invitation to me to attend the set a marginal validity which I was relieved to possess.

At last, a third scene was ready to be shot—the Jewish valuer empties a bag of what he thinks is jewelry and finds himself contemplating human teeth. Spielberg gave the actor involved a complex set of eye and head movements to perform. Look down in shock and disbelief. Recover quickly with the realization that such reactions might bring danger. Look to the left, look to the right. And then contemplate, in a more measured and despairing way, and with an infinite sadness, the gold-filled teeth again.

And thus the morning's work was concluded, and we ate in the actors' and crew's tent with everyone else, Spielberg taking the same place each day. It was wonderful to see Poles well-fed, too, since Polish citizens had been so scrawny in 1981, and everyone knew that even in the new democratic system, access to food was irregular.

Even at meals Spielberg was always asking questions. He liked having people around to discuss things with, even while the technicians changed the lighting or the camera crew set up for a new shot. Many of the survivors who visited the set were astonished by the extent of the questions Spielberg asked them. Part of his strength as a director, says Palowski, was his willingness to seek input from just about anyone who had any connection with the story.

Spielberg told me about the sundry former prisoners he had had on set, and whom he would soon be seeing in Jerusalem for the shooting of the scene in which various survivors place a stone on Schindler's grave. He had typically questioned them at length. When pressed to comment on the footage, they told him that everyone among the actors playing prisoners looked too well-dressed and too well-fed, except that they knew that if he reproduced the reality of their camp life, the viewer would be appalled and alienated. The thing he couldn't reproduce anyhow, they said, was the stench of the camp, of their own starved bodies, of the latrines too, and of the bodies moldering close to the surface of the soil on Chujowa Górka, Prick Hill.

That afternoon, in a small building near the Liban chalk quarry, the scene was shot in which Schindler goes to the Jewish family who were his partners but who had, in his opinion, taken too much merchandise. Only Kaminski and his crew and the actors could fit into the room. The rest of us, Spielberg included, watched the scene on monitors in the open. It was one which richly illustrated the ambiguity of Oskar's character early in the war; but in the end, purely for the needs of brevity, it would not make the film's final cut.

Next we went to the Liban chalk quarry above which had been built Starski's version of Amon Goeth's villa. One descended by stairwells into the chalk pit, which had been transformed into the Płaszów camp. During the war, this quarry had been a penal camp, and still felt like it. All the unused industrial iron hoppers and other equipment kept station, along with Amon, on that merciless shelf above the camp. It was, in its own right, a wonderful set.

I realized that I had used too much film taking snapshots and would run out, but the location photographer, David James, an Englishman who had taken stills on many film sets, gave my daughter and me one of his rolls of black and white so that we could take photographs on the same terms as Janusz Kaminski was filming. Indeed, most of the filming my daughter Jane and I saw occurred here, at this all too credible version of Płaszów. We saw the scene of a conference between Amon Goeth and Itzhak Stern, and a brutal encounter between Lisiek, the servant boy and groom, and Goeth over Lisiek's supposed mistreatment of a saddle. We would see Lisiek shot, as had happened in the real Płaszów, by the sniper rifle of Amon Goeth, firing from his balcony, bare-chested, a cigarette in his mouth. The scene was just like a photo the Austrian factory manager Raimund Titsch had taken of Goeth during the war, a photo bought from Titsch by Poldek in 1963. The mother of young Wojciech Klata, the actor playing Lisiek, was very upset about a splinter of gravel which went into the boy's eye from an explosion set off among the dirt on the floor of the pit, but it would happily prove to be an insignificant injury.

The assistant cameraman's mother from Boston turned up and glowed at her son's success, so proud that he was shooting this film.

There was a luxury coach that served as a sort of club bus, to which the producers, the executive producer, the director, Bonnie Curtis and others could have access, and where they could rest free from harassment. A little jet-lagged, I had recourse to the club bus during the afternoon, and fell into conversation with Jerry Molen, a genial man who looked like a wise uncle in a Western. Molen, this gentle but firm and experienced man, was Steven's gatekeeper. He did not lie, nor did he mind the task. In his view, it was important that Steven concentrate on the job.

Eighteen

Among the actors my daughter Jane and I met was the greatly
talented Caroline Goodall, whose role was that of Emilie
Schindler. Caroline and her husband were also remarkably
fine company. We took to going to a restaurant in Slawkowska
Street, just off the town center and obviously the former town-
house of a noble family. The restaurant combined excellent
food with rough Bulgarian wine. Ben Kingsley and his English
girlfriend often joined Jane and myself, and Caroline and her
husband. Neither Kingsley nor Goodall put on thespian airs,
and Kingsley loved conversation and ideas. On one of our visits to the old *palais* which housed the restaurant, students
from the Kraków Conservatorium came in and performed the
music of the now vanished ghetto of Kazimierz.

I tried to watch the rushes each night before setting off to
the town square. Ralph Fiennes, accompanying us one night,
told us that during a forthcoming long weekend he had
Steven's permission to fly to New York, his first visit there, and

audition for the role of the young Charles Van Doren in *Quiz Show*, a film about the quiz scandals which ruined the Van Doren name in the late 1950s.

Indeed, this was the only long weekend break of the shoot, and actors and technicians were making plans for it. On the location at the Liban quarry, the Croatian caterer told me that he was going to use the weekend to go home to Zagreb. It astonished me once again that Europe was so intimately small. If I journeyed westward from Sydney for the same time as he was going to be driving overnight from Kraków, I would still not be out of the state of New South Wales. On the Friday before the weekend, I mentioned to Spielberg what a shock it was for me to find that it was worthwhile driving from Kraków to Zagreb for a long weekend, as the caterer intended to do.

The Balkans were in the news then; another instance of Europe's capacity for great hate in little space. Spielberg said that this was a good time to be making the film—it was the first time since World War II that the term "ethnic cleansing" was being unapologetically used, by, among other people, Slobodan Milošević, then president of Serbia. Authors and filmmakers sometimes like to add these genuine, more elevated hopes to what they do. In reality, it is proven over and over that, although we can identify with historic injustice, under present racial pressures it is the vomit most of us can't wait to get back to, and that's the human tragedy.

That weekend my daughter Jane and I decided we would go to Auschwitz, which she had never seen. Jerzy was willing to drive us there in the car the producers had kindly provided.

My daughter in particular had made friends with Geno Lech-
ner, the young, angular German who played the role of Amon's
mistress, Majola. (There was within the villa a bedroom set up
where, in one scene, we had seen her and Amon lie together
languidly and from which Amon emerged, in his underwear,
to bring down summary judgment on some poor creature in
the camp.) Geno wanted to come to Auschwitz too. In bright
spring daylight Jerzy drove us out through farmland and
forests to the town of Katowice, and then through the somewhat smaller but equally normal-looking town of Oświęcim
which had given its German transliteration, Auschwitz, to the
notorious camp. I had been this way before, but for Geno and
Jane it was a new road. They took in the landscape with particular interest and, on such a pleasing day, the chatter with Jerzy
was jokey and lightly teasing. Then, in the midst of grass and
woods and wildflowers, we encountered the grim gate and
walls of Auschwitz 1, which declared that work would make its
inmates free.

I found it all the harder a place to enter in this vivid spring
than it had been when I visited it last time with Poldek in a
dour late winter. The contrast between the intensity of the season and the deathliness of the place shocked us profoundly. In
Auschwitz 1 they used to hang and beat people, confine prisoners in boxes and hutches barely big enough for a human to
breathe within, and experiment with human organs. It was
one of the compression cells, where the prisoner had barely
room to move or air to breathe, which set Geno weeping.

But she insisted she wanted to see all of it, and so we went on to tour Auschwitz 2, Auschwitz-Birkenau, the full-scale, vast *Vernichtungslager*. Here, within the deal-thin walls of the prison huts, we felt the suddenly penetrative air, even of the spring. We extended our journey into the gas chambers, an experience I had found most testing last time I was here. After we had put ourselves through it, we strolled out that infamous railway gate, part of the iconography of twentieth-century horror, and got in Jerzy's car and rolled back pensively between green pastures toward Kraków, trying to make small talk to a stark-eyed Geno.

The climatic luck didn't always work for Steven. Since spring was now quite advanced, he needed to get the Kraków fire department to make foam for a scene requiring snow. The location is meant to be Brinnlitz, the site of Oskar's second camp. Oskar goes to the local parish church, outside a beautiful Austro-Hungarian Empire church with a reredos and elegant dome, to ask the priest to sell him the ground for the Goleszów cattle-truck people to be buried in as Jews. Jane and I stood by banks of foam, visited the church, lit a candle for my parents—they were consoled by candles lit for them anywhere in strange and remote places. But this scene would not make the final cut. It was one of Oskar's subtler mercies and in the end was seen as a side issue to the general forward thrust of the man.

Jane and I had a last dinner with the splendid Ben Kingsley and his girlfriend, then prepared to leave Kraków after two weeks on the set. I was grateful we had not been made to feel marginal to the film, and we had been treated as germane members of the tribe of filmmakers through the habitual courtesy of Spielberg, Bonnie Curtis and Jerry Molen. From London I caught the plane back to California and another seminar, another workshop. But very soon UCI commencement arrived in the leafy, clear-aired Southern California spring, and so we were packing again, a process that was getting to be tedious. Back to Australia after all that excitement, I brought my rather astonishing melange of photographs of Eritrean polling booths, and of film sets in Kazimierz and Płaszów.

I was still working on my novel set in my grandparents' Australia, 1900, when my lanky, dreamy grandfather and small dumpling-esque grandmother had settled on the north coast of New South Wales in a river valley. I was also deeply involved in research on Irish convicts, and their world of crimes that the occupying British authority saw merely as crimes against property, but which were, in fact, crimes of politics, however inchoate.

These stories now occupied my days, as I heard little of the Oskar film, of how it had edited up. Poldek called and told me in an appalled voice that he had heard from Sid Sheinberg that Universal intended to release the film in twenty-nine screens throughout the United States. "I said to him, Sid, I ask you: *Twenty-nine screens?* He said to me, Holocaust films are hard, so we're going to get good word of mouth going on this film, that's why. I said, Word of mouth? For a Steven Spielberg film?" But Sheinberg had told Poldek that Holocaust films had to work that way. It had never been otherwise. They weren't popular. Poldek answered him, "So *The Diary of Anne Frank* isn't popular? So *Judgment at Nuremberg* is Donald Duck? I told Sid," continued Poldek, "that this was the great story of humanity man to man, and the world is ready to hear it and see it. But he said, If that's the way it is, Poldek, the people will find it. A crazy way of doing business!"

I have to say that having seen something of the quality of the film, this news was a little disappointing. In all the multiplexes from Maine to Louisiana, from Washington State to the East Coast, it would have no place. In all the small residual town cinemas that showed "art house" films, a term generally reserved for British or European or Australian films, or for esoteric American ones or the latest Hungarian or Czech hit—even in these places, it would have a limited and muted voice.

By the time the Australian winter ended, I had returned to the University of California and found, as soon as I arrived, that Poldek's concerns about limited release had been largely allayed. The word was out in the film community and among the media that *Schindler's List* was a startling film. I did my interview for the current affairs show *20/20*'s tribute to Poldek, itself an index of the intense prerelease interest, which extended even to the story of how Poldek and I had met, and how Poldek's stalwart soul had got things going. "So you'd never heard of this guy Schindler before?" interviewers always asked me. A new edition of *Schindler's Ark/List* made an appearance and, happily for the Keneallys, it became a habitual presence on the *New York Times Book Review* paperback bestseller list in its far-from-cheap trade paperback edition.

My mother was about to turn eighty, and in November 1993 we dashed back to Sydney for the celebration at my brother Johnny's place in Gladesville. My mother had been a potent force in both our lives; she had been ambitious for us and always undaunted in the years my father was absent in Africa. By the date of her birthday, I had not yet seen the final cut, the cinema-exhibition version, of the film, but the brilliant trailer, with no commentary, produced awe in viewers, and indeed in me, while also filling me with an obscure fear that I might not be able to handle, accommodate, absorb the scale of it when I saw it.

We got an amused call the day before my mother's party from Bonnie Curtis, Spielberg's aide. "Where are you guys?" she asked. "We've been looking for you all over California. We want to fly you to the premiere in Washington on Monday night. The president's coming."

My mother's party was to be an afternoon-to-early-evening affair, and it was worked out that if Judy and I flew to America on the Sunday evening of the party—our daughter Jane insisted on coming too—we would be in Washington late on the American Sunday. The dateline gave us that bonus. Thus, we would have to leave my mother's party just before it came to a close—the talkative and boozy nature of our clan ensured that all parties went late into the night—but after the tribal ceremonials and greetings to which she was entitled. The only thing was, we would have to take our luggage with us to the party.

On this exceptional Sabbath, Universal sent a car to transport us to the party and then the airport, and since my parents also lived on the northern beaches of Sydney, we could collect them on the way through. So my mother arrived at her party in an unaccustomed stretch limo, an improbable form of delivery for a girl from the bush—as she still saw herself. There was a mass of relatives in Johnny's backyard and in the rooms that faced it on that overcast afternoon. In the late afternoon, after the cake had been cut and presents given, the relatives all waved us off in the exorbitance of the hired car.

I thought that all this, the two first-class air tickets and the rest, was characteristic of Steven's generosity of soul. There was no necessity to have Judy and me there in Washington. In my role as a crazy workaholic, I can remember writing up some of my Irish files for the big book on prisoners and their world, even as we flew at the kinder end of the aircraft. But sleep claimed us too. Perhaps among the most discombobulating air journeys in the world is the one from Sydney to the East Coast of the United States. Hours of lost time zones are so scattered in the plane's wake that morning becomes night in short order, and night morning.

The dusk arrival from Dulles airport in Washington at the Four Seasons in Georgetown was nonetheless like a homecoming. Liam Neeson was there, Janusz Kaminski was wearing a suit. Jerry Molen, Branko Lustig, the shy and now famous Ralph Fiennes, and Poldek and Misia—they had all arrived earlier in the day. We grabbed a light evening meal in the coffee shop with Misia and Poldek, and Poldek was, justifiably enough, glowing with his success. "So he tells me twenty-nine screens. It was always going to be a thousand times twenty-nine!"

"You two did it," said Misia. "Before the actors, before Steven, you two were there."

Misia's compliment was too great a claim for me to bear. I had not seen the film. I did not even know what the time was. I was still both delighted and very afraid.

As for Poldek, he made an appreciative growl. There were some in his own community who said he'd done it all along for the money, but his rewards had been modest in reality, and had taken him away from his business, which had frequently been in a perilous condition. Whatever admixture of vanity there was in his loyalty to Schindler—and there is in every good act such an admixture—his stubborn resistance to letting the tale die seemed genuinely heroic. He had now done the job which had been perhaps his chief agenda item since he first settled in Beverly Hills nearly forty years before. There was a little more of the banter: "Well, it's your determination, Poldek." "Yes, Thomas, but determination on its own is nothing." Such was the nervous conversational tennis of a wonderful, edgy evening. Misia softly rejoiced in both our credits and said, in her quiet but authoritative way, "It's a very, very good film, Tom." It was only much later that I thought, She must know. She was, after all, a woman who had suffered through it in her young life, culminating in the six to eight hundred calories of Auschwitz cuisine, and the intimacy of death. She must know.

The premiere would be the following night at a theater in Georgetown. No one would wear dinner suits, searchlights would not probe the sky, lasers would not dart, and the normal red-carpet traipse would be eschewed. President Clinton and his remarkable, much admired and much maligned wife would attend, but there would be no formal lineup of stars with an exultant public looking on.

On the morning of the premiere, a Monday, a special screening had been arranged for Judy, Jane, me and a journalist from *Time* magazine. We met up in the empty foyer, and then sat ourselves in the middle of the empty cinema, two thirds of the way back from the screen in an immense vacancy of seats. The emptiness made me uneasy about the coming viewing, and the fact that the *Time* man would ask me questions. It was a long time since I had written the book, and thus a long time since I had read it, and in terms of images and brutality I was both familiar but also unfamiliar with the material.

As the film ran and reached the scenes of the liquidation of the ghetto, I was, in a way, gasping for breath. The people I watched on the screen were in a terrible flux of history, in a mincer, a shredder of dreams and attachments. And at the climax of the night massacre of those who hid during the liquidation, an officer finds an old piano and plays Mozart. The question was always this: Why was this barbarity enacted by the agents of Europe's high culture? Why were the SS *Einsatzgruppen* full of philosophy and theology graduates, pastors? At first sight the brutality of the SS seems a denial of Europe's cultural triumph and of the value of its urbanity. And yet the higher a culture is, the more refined its identity, the easier it becomes to deny any value to other identities. High Europe always played at ethnic contempt because it *was* High Europe, and so had the strength, the authority, to make the racial rules. We great unwashed of the outer world, on the coasts of new continents, though we might ourselves have behaved atrociously to indigenes, were baffled by the determination with which Europe returned to the frenzies of racial myth. Nice boys and not-so-nice boys took up the theme, put on the uniform, did the dirty work.

In the film's narrative, Oskar's career developed effortlessly from these beginnings; the filmmakers lacked the leisure to explore Emilie's own motivations in detail. Under the necessities of editing, the latter part of the film, in which the story of Schindler's second camp in Brinnlitz is told, seemed inevitably foreshortened. The fact that the camp produced no munitions could, on film, tell only half the story. The other half was that the camp operated entirely and profitably on the black market.

The Schindler film was the first Holocaust film up to that time, with the possible exception of *Europa Europa*, to deliver the viewer safe at the end. By comparison with *Schindler's List*, the later *Life Is Beautiful* seemed to me nothing but an extended and fairly tasteless joke. If the Nazis could be survived by looking at them under the rubric of comedy, a race with a gift for comedy would have done it and survived.

The performances in the Schindler film were such as to make me forget that I had once broken bread, or the seals on bottles of rough Bulgarian red wine, with these folk. I felt that the emphatically ambiguous Schindler of the early part of the film was exactly the Schindler Spielberg needed to create, stressing his opportunism strongly to make the point that this man had not come to Kraków in the first place to save anyone. Spielberg once told me that movies were required to take account of the bladders of filmgoers. His did not, but it was almost as if his film had the power to suspend human limits of concentration for the time it ran.

Late in the film, on the point of departure from his prisoners, Schindler speaks of how he might have saved more had he thought to sell a badge or a Mercedes. The reality was that, as many of his former prisoners testified, they were already concerned that the camp had reached full capacity—he had taken in the Goleszów people, for example. And although the departure scene made infallible movie sense, it seemed to undermine his own rationality, as if the idea of saving more prisoners had only just come to him then, in the last hours of war. I later mentioned this reservation to the *Time* journalist, when he asked me what I thought of the film, and he made rather a lot of it. Overall, it was obvious that the picture was an extraordinary piece of film craft, and that it took people as close to the reality of regimented racism and its results as one could without losing a mass audience. Indeed, it was not until the lights came up that I remembered where we were, that we were in a Washington cinema toward noon on an overcast

Monday, with my daughter whispering, "Wasn't that great?" I had not remembered that once I wrote this material as a book. The length of time had distanced me, made me forget much. Now it was all back.

I had enjoyed in a particular, personal way seeing those I had interviewed long ago making their way past Schindler's grave, laying their stones there, and Mrs. Schindler with the actress who played her, my friend Caroline Goodall. The survivors who had been young when I wrote the book were now middle-aged, and the middle-aged now elderly, and for some inexpressible reason I found the passage of time, and how it had left them, touching and triumphant despite all the blood and despoliation of the Second World War. That morning I was at the same time both daunted and excited that I would see the film again soon. Indeed, that very evening.

Altogether, the fact that I had been permitted to view the film prior to the premiere seemed to me a symbol of how casually generous Spielberg could be; for all he knew, I might have denounced the film beforehand and produced a small scandal, which would have affected the film neither one way nor the other ultimately, but which could have been fatuously wounding in the short term. In any case, I could not help but be cheered that he knew that would not happen.

Nineteen

That night we were all back at the same cinema, in suits. Our workaday look acknowledged the frightful deaths, the years of terror that had gone into making the tale. The same mixture of dizziness and dread possessed me. Nonetheless, I reenacted with Branko Lustig the early scene of the movie in which Liam Neeson hands Branko a roll of money, offering him a fold of dollars while Judy took a picture. The president and his wife came and shook hands with everyone vigorously and in rapid order, speaking in low tones. Though not always popular in America, he was much admired in the outer world and extremely popular in Australia. Hillary Clinton mentioned to me a book Nan Talese had sent her—*Woman of the Inner Sea*—for which she claimed an enthusiasm. The Clintons were clearly close friends of Spielberg, who was an energetic supporter of their broader politics. At the end of the screening, people did not know whether to clap or gasp. Once the applause began, it became a frenzy.

It fell to Judy, the great-granddaughter of an Irish political prisoner and a Limerick shoplifter, to approach the manager, standing in place to bow to the departing president in the quickly emptying foyer, and ask what was going to happen to the film poster in the display case at the front of the cinema. He said calmly, "I just take it down for now. Would you like it?" Hence, as an afterthought, the Keneallys acquired that premiere poster.

Then we all went back to the hotel. We sat reflectively over some wine. No post-premiere bash had been staged to mute the impact. Steven Spielberg signed a copy of the book for me. Jerry Molen spoke softly. He had seen many nights like this. Murmuring reverentially, we relived the black and white polarities of terror and deliverance, and the grays of ghetto-style and camp squalor. Even by now, midnight on Monday, November 26, 1993, the film was a triumph.

But despite its success in translating the icons of the Holocaust into accessible form, there was that in me which still said, "Film is just so limited." I was, of course, delighted that within the terms of popular cinema, Spielberg had portrayed so successfully the tale the survivors had once told me. Yet there was also something in me which remained, and indeed still remains, fundamentally unimpressed by cinema as compared to writing. Needless to say, this is more my problem than the cinema's.

It was clear that though the film was destined for broad approval, it raised passionate questions too. How could the Holocaust be adequately depicted in a "Hollywood" film?

asked some historians and film critics. Was it decent to try to do so? Wasn't the Holocaust untranslatable in conventional film terms? Some declared the film to be a form of Nazi gangster movie which was far outshone by Claude Lanzmann's 1985 documentary *Shoah*. The reaction of African American students at Castlemont High School in Oakland who laughed at the execution of a woman engineer—they believed a body shot in such a way would fall otherwise than it did—was gleefully reported in the media. In those early days it seemed that the world was trying to make up its mind whether it would award *Schindler* the full laurels.

In a symposium reproduced in the *Village Voice* involving Art Spiegelman, the creator of the brilliant *Maus* cartoons; filmmaker Ken Jacobs; and the admirable Philip Gourevitch, who would later tell the story of the Rwandan hecatomb, there were a lot of harsh opinions uttered about the film, even by those who defended Spielberg's right to make it. It is probably worth quoting Spiegelman's both extreme and contradictory view:

> These Jews are slightly gentrified versions of Julius Streicher's *Der Stürmer* caricatures: the juiceless Jewish accountant, the Jewish seductress, and, most egregiously, the Jews bargaining and doing business inside a church. It's one of the few scenes that wasn't even borrowed from the novel. Spielberg has long had a Jewish problem. The Jewish "magic" which leaped out of the Lost Ark at the end of his first *Raiders* movie

was all the wrath of God melting down the villains with a supernatural nuclear bomb. *Schindler's List* refracts the Holocaust through the central image of a righteous Gentile in a world of Jewish bit players and extras. The Jews function as an occasion for Christian redemption.

One critic argued that to have the music score relate to the burning of bodies on Chujowa Górka was a form of manipulation. It was as if Spielberg had been the only filmmaker ever to employ a composer, and stood condemned for doing so. Others asked, with more justice, Why would there not be a score? There is always a score in movies. And why, in such a scene, was it manipulative? Yet, as another critic said, "It's all done in movie terms . . . It's saturated with movieness . . . It seems a little strange to attack him for fulfilling that function, where if he did something else you would be ignoring him."

The morning after the premiere, we visited as a group the recently opened Holocaust Memorial Museum in Washington. Mrs. Schindler, whom I had seen only on film and communicated with only by mail, was a member of the group, seated in a wheelchair and accompanied by her companion, the Argentinian woman Erika Rosenberg. She looked frail but retained her handsome face—she, too, had participated in what Poldek had thought of as the bounty of bone structure. She wore a grandmotherly half-smile and glittering eyes. I went up to her and complimented her in rudimentary German for being there, in the foyer of the museum which commemorated the massive events in which she had had an heroic part. The vigor in her eyes could be attributed in part to the fact that she was still fighting her corner of her ruinous marriage to Oskar. The new eminence the rascal had acquired was hard for her to bear; that much was apparent. To an extent, and even understandably, she would never stop disliking Poldek for running with the story, me for writing it, Spielberg for exalting it on film.

We toured the museum and looked at the photographs and exhibits and, on video screens, the survivors invoking Sobibor, Mauthausen, Treblinka, Auschwitz. Exhibitions showed the interiors of Eastern European Jewish homes, and one told the story of a Jewish child's experience of the Holocaust, related in a way which had gained the approval, an attendant told us, of three child psychiatrists.

We experienced the inside of a cattle truck, and it fascinated me to see people who were all familiar with the insides of such rough transport peering in and frowning. Emilie herself knew from the Goleszów men what the inside of a truck was like. Poldek and Misia certainly knew, and Misia graciously saved us from the news that experiences suffered on the lip of the grave might be only faintly reproduced in a Washington museum.

At some stage about now, Spielberg got the idea of raising a team of volunteers throughout the world to interview all remaining survivors of the Holocaust, and to record their experiences on a database archive. It would be an extraordinary database, where one could both listen to and look at live testimonies of survivors, but also cross-reference them to build a picture of particular aspects of ghetto and camp life, from ghetto police to food rations to SS NCOs. It would be a repository for future generations. The value of such a database for researchers would be prodigious. I couldn't help asking myself what it would be like to have such a database of Irish Famine survivors, or of victims of the slave trade to North America and the West Indies. But Spielberg also wanted to lay the remaining testimony down for the reason that the Holocaust had happened to what he now saw as *his people*.

He intended to call this operation the Shoah Foundation, and it soon began its life in prefabricated offices close to Amblin and Universal's car park.

Poldek and I visited the place a number of times, as it grew and took on a gradually more formal appearance.

Using the database, one could not only access the story of any given survivor, but if one wanted to check, for example, on the population of rats in the Lodz ghetto, one had only to type in the request and the search engine would surrender everything survivors could tell you about the unsanitary conditions of Lodz.

The day after the Washington premiere, the film was to be shown in New York to raise money for Glovin's Schindler Foundation. This had been a condition of Glovin's signature to the contract all those years before. The entire Schindler entourage, including the leading actors, were to be at this event.

Thus Emilie was in New York too, and appeared on a number of television shows. And always, the handsome, middle-aged Erika Rosenberg pushed the idea that here was the true source of Oskar's altruism. And yet she'd been cut out of everything and gone utterly uncompensated! Rosenberg would tell the world, "She [Emilie] was cut out of the film and the book in a very humiliating and offensive way." Since Spielberg had expressed great admiration for Emilie, I knew she had not been treated offensively. I got an impression of tranquillity from Emilie, while Rosenberg fibrillated around her, making claims of which the world would, in months to come, take notice.

The afternoon of the New York premiere, Judy and I called at Simon & Schuster, who were so pleased with the book that they intended to bring out a new hardcover edition, a kind of special-occasion presentation volume. To celebrate, like a suddenly flush miner from the Australian gold rushes, I bought Judy a gold bracelet with *Amor Vincit Omnia* engraved on it.

Irvin Glovin, in a splendid dinner suit which fitted his tennis player's form magnificently, and Jeannie, with her California tan and cocktail dress, made impressive figures that night in the foyer of the theater. They gave us a warm welcome. They told us that there was a party back in their suite at the Waldorf-Astoria that night, but genuinely enough we claimed exhaustion. I had recently resigned from the board of the Schindler Foundation, rendered uneasy by Glovin's intentions to endow researchers to find from the study of Schindler's life a virtual inoculation for interracial cruelty. They seemed very disappointed, and I promised them I would visit them the next day and have a drink with them. I was not surprised that the Schindler Foundation failed to ever set up its research project. It may have been that presidents and vice-chancellors of universities were as disturbed as I was by the fixity of Glovin's ideas.

Now, at Steven's invitation, we were flown to London for the premiere there. It possessed more of the character of an accustomed premiere, with a carpet outside the cinema in Leicester Square, and a large cocktail party beforehand. Here I saw among the crowd the lively Australian Kathy Lette and her extraordinary husband, also an Australian, the human rights advocate and brilliant lawyer Geoffrey Robertson, one of the most remarkable fellows, the most learned, the most logically gifted advocates one could meet. And there was their embattled friend and mine, Salman Rushdie, whom Judy and I had first met when we attended the Booker Prize ceremony the year after *Schindler's Ark* had won it.

Spielberg had also invited Judy, Jane and myself to the Viennese premiere; indeed, to the Frankfurt and Tel Aviv premieres as well, if we wished to accompany him. But my seminar and lecture responsibilities limited us to Vienna.

There was some anxiety among the Spielberg camp about Vienna. A neo-Nazi letter bomb had recently blown off part of the Mayor of Vienna's hand. And when Judy, Jane and I arrived at the Hotel Sacher a little later than the rest of the Spielberg group, and tried to register at the normal check-in desk, the studio's security people descended upon us, surrounded us like sheepdogs and urged us to come with them and not to loiter in reception. We were given badges to identify us—in this case the badge of the day represented the Great Seal of the State of California. We were to wear it at all times. Anyone who did not have such a badge would be kept separate from us by phalanxes of security. The third floor was devoted entirely to Spielberg's party, and a guard with a semiautomatic sat before the two ornate lifts which serviced the floor.

That afternoon we assembled and were led via service lifts through the kitchen into a basement corridor, up steps and then into an ornate hall which had been set up for a press conference. Among us was Simon Wiesenthal, the Nazi hunter, who had come to join us on the rostrum and with whom I had a little time to chat, with appropriate awe. At that time Wiesenthal was elderly but unstooped, and looked much younger than his years. I knew that he was aware of Oskar's case, and he told me he had met both Poldek and Oskar earlier in the century.

On the rostrum I sat with Spielberg, Branko Lustig and Simon Wiesenthal during the press conference, in the midst of which one irate Austrian journalist asked Spielberg why he had called the film *Schindler's List* rather than *Schindler's Ark*. Because *Schindler's List* is the title I bought, he answered with justifiable bemusement. When the reporters inquired about Oskar, Wiesenthal confirmed that he had met him and had admired his work, and lamented that resistance to the process of extermination had not been more widespread. He approved of Oskar's Righteous Persons status.

Jane and Judy had watched the conference in progress from
the back of the hall. When, after a considerable time, a halt was
called, a stampede of press, uncharacteristic of Austrians,
came pressing forward, seeking further interviews. A fighting
phalanx of American and Austrian security men—themselves
adorned with the Great Seal badge—ruthlessly pushed aside
the press to enable the members of our party at the back of the
room to reach us at the front. It was an extraordinarily powerful performance and reminded me of the rolling maul in
rugby. And so we escaped by a further door, down staff corridors and offices and through more kitchens, until we arrived
in a laneway behind the Sacher, where three Mercedes and a
number of other vehicles waited for us to make up a convoy.

We were hustled into the Mercedes and whisked away at a
great pace—no gradual takeoff. The security men in each vehi-
cle communicated via the radios in their sleeves as we sped
beneath the wan sun toward the Austrian chancellory. We drew
up in a baroque archway and were urgently told to leave the
cars. I followed my daughter Jane up a stone spiral staircase,
the type the servants of Count Metternich or Talleyrand had
once used—the tradesmen's entrance. A bulky bodyguard in
front of my daughter dropped a huge, squarish semiautomatic
pistol out of his suit onto the step. It made a metallic clunk and
lay on the step ahead like a suddenly assertive animal. *"Scusi,"*
said the man, and he scooped it up, concealed it back in his
suit again with one smooth movement, and continued to climb
the stairs.

In the corner of a huge office, and beneath great moldings

and decorative paintings, we were greeted by Chancellor Franz Vranitzky, a dark-haired, good-looking man in early middle-age. He led us to a low table there and we all sat down around it. He talked to us about the way the war had been followed by the mythology that the Holocaust was all a German work, and how the issue of Austrian participation was suppressed, since to utter it would be to divide citizens. He had written a graduate thesis on this, to the chagrin of some of his academic advisers.

We were all encouraged to talk, and when it was my turn I spoke of the patterns of replies to the queries I had made of *Schindlerjuden*. I remarked it was also a matter of amazement that Schindler's behavior had not been more influenced by the state's conditioning of German opinion. The license to hate was writ very broadly, and one would normally have expected someone like Oskar, no philosopher, to have adopted it uncritically. Better qualified, more intellectual men than himself had done so. Otto Ohlendorf, who commanded one of the *Einsatzgruppen*, had studied jurisprudence and economics at Leipzig, Göttingen and Padua. Ernst Biberstein, another officer, was a Protestant pastor. Another a physician, another an opera singer. I felt I was struggling in my remarks—the recent timetable hadn't been good for thinking—and I believed that I had let Spielberg down a bit by having little to say that was original. Everything I said here was either in the book or in articles I had written.

When we had all spoken, the genial chancellor told his story of the rise of neo-Nazism in Austria, assured us of our safety, and then asked, "Would you like to see the room where the Congress of Vienna occurred?" And by the shortest of corridors, we now entered a glittering hall of mirrors and brocaded and embellished surfaces. Here, after the Napoleonic Wars, a conservative peace had been made which had sustained the Austro-Hungarian Empire for another hundred years and produced the so-called *Pax Britannica*, the British Peace, in which there were no European wars, though many others were fought in the acquisition and retention of colonies.

It was late afternoon by now, and we enjoyed another car chase to the American embassy in Boltzmanngasse. The splendor of this eighteenth-century house seemed like a more warmly decorated continuation of the chancellory. We met Swanee Grace Hunt, the then U.S. ambassador and a member of the fabled Texas Hunt family, who at one stage—so I seem to remember—had cornered the world silver market and so, unlike the Keneallys, had never been short of a dollar. Spielberg approached me once we were all in the room where cocktails were served. He said, "Will you do me a favor? You were good at the chancellory. Will you make the speech for me?" The idea scared me less than had the impromptu speech at the chancellory. Once I got up I simply told our story, the story of all the film's progenitors, including Poldek. Thanks to generations of talkative Keneallys, the speech was made, and I could have a scotch.

I fell into conversation with Mrs. Bankier and her daughter. Bankier himself, now deceased, was the man who had run Rekord, as it was called before it became Schindler's Emalia and DEF. Abraham Bankier was either a part-owner or related to the owners, and was a hero as universally beloved as Stern or Pemper. But in the film these three characters had been coalesced into Stern, and a wistfulness over that—I would not say a resentment—possessed Mrs. Bankier as she and her daughter spoke of ways to make some appropriate gesture to her husband's memory. I told her to quote anything from the book that she wished to. "I realize that this is what movies do," said the daughter.

The cinema, when we got there for the premiere, was in chaos, and Judy, Jane and I were manhandled to our seats by a muscular security woman yelling, *"Der Buchautor!"* Spielberg spoke briefly onstage, then Wiesenthal, and as the film began we departed from the back row of the cinema—we were by now familiar with the film—along an obscure corridor again, and off for a splendid dinner in a traditional Austrian restaurant. One of the members of the party was Béatrice Macola, who had played Schindler's girlfriend Ingrid in the film. Spielberg, no wine drinker, asked Jane, Béatrice and myself for help choosing the wine; a boy from barbarous Sydney helping a boy from Cleveland with the high vintages of Europe.

For us, that dinner was one of farewell. The Spielberg team were pulling out for Frankfurt the next morning. Spielberg embraced Jane as we came to the service lift in the basement of the Sacher, and to my amazement Judy, too, asked to be hugged—it was rarely she asked such a gesture of film people. I told Spielberg to feel honored.

When our breakfast arrived the next morning, we found the

floor very quiet, in an unearthly silence now that the solemn circus had departed. We still possessed our now irrelevant badges, sans man with semiautomatic, and, since I was to do a book-signing that morning, I still had an excursion to make in a town which was reputedly full of neo-Nazis. We descended to the concierge and asked the way to the bookstore, and thus walked out into a biting morning and urbane streets full of fascinating stores, past the huge Plague memorial, toward the bookshop we were to visit. It was a brilliant movie-set of a *Buchhandlung*, suffused with the amber light from gleaming windows. The restrained and artful spines of European books displayed themselves so gracefully. The proprietor and I spoke of the Australian writer Europeans liked best, Patrick White, the great Nobel Prize–winning novelist.

A few people arrived, and were shy, but at last there formed a queue which grew apace. But when I began to sign, it was not a case of combative neo-Nazis, but of young Viennese coming forward, university students and young couples who, to my astonishment, wept when I signed. I mentioned the tears to the bookshop proprietor. "They've never heard about it in accessible form before," he said. "Their parents never talked about it."

I made the obvious point to him that these young readers were not to blame.

"It's the shock of knowing we were in it too. We tended to put it off on the Germans."

Having unwittingly generated such reactions in Austrian youth, I was pleased not to have to face the test of Frankfurt.

In the months to come, my skepticism about whether the film might influence people was allayed, in part at least, particularly by the young who wanted their books signed. I found that Hispanic, ethnic Chinese, Filipinos, Koreans and Californian Japanese related strongly to the book. They had a memory of being stereotyped in childhood, as did the subcontinental Indian community in America, presenting the book for signature at this or that Barnes & Noble, from Thousand Oaks to the Mexican border.

There is very little of narrative value in the consequent honors that come a writer's way purely on the basis that a good film has been made of a book the writer has written, but I remember one of them with particular affection. It was a collegial event, the Scripter Awards, in the library of the University of Southern California, attended by Spielberg and the other producers, at which Zaillian and I accepted a prize conjointly. I remember the appearance of Poldek on *Larry King*. Poldek showed he had learned something about television since our days with Jane Pauley. I remember, too, a pre-Oscars party hosted by Joe Segal, a Century City magnate, and Kaye Kimberly-Clark, his Australian-born wife and legendary beauty. They wanted the centerpiece to be a huge Oskar cake. The cast of *Schindler* flocked to the party, as did Jane Campion, who had been nominated for the Academy Award for her film *The Piano*, and Toni Colette of *Muriel's Wedding*, and other Australians. The artwork which astonished us all was not the cake, but the pictures on Joe Segal's walls—the Légers, the Picassos and, as Liam Neeson said, "The fookin' Cézannes, man! Have you seen the fookin' Cézannes?" Liam similarly appreciated the deeply gold-plated lavatory seat, washbasin and taps. But what astonished me was to meet one of the Segals' neighbors, Rhonda Fleming, star in my childhood of *The Spiral Staircase*, and of Hitchcock's *Spellbound*. She was so agelessly beautiful in her early seventies that the question of whether knives had played any part seemed utterly improper. Poldek and I took home the chocolate Oscars we had been allotted, and deposited them in our refrigerators, where even in Australia mine still resides.

But then, among the most memorable contingent honors of the season, came an invitation to the White House for dinner. Judy drove up from University Hills to the Newport Beach mall to buy me an Armani dinner suit at Neiman Marcus, which the people at the university generally referred to as "Needless Markup." I would look swish in the White House, or so my wife's theory went. Judy and Jane flew to Washington and booked earlier in the day into the Willard Hotel, the most resonatingly famous of all Washington hotels, where Thomas Francis Meagher, one of the Australian convicts I was researching, had always stayed. In the meantime I gave my afternoon seminar.

Rushing back to University Hills, I packed, went to the airport and arrived at last at dusk in that hotel in Washington so closely associated with presidents, generals, writers and other riffraff. I took what I thought was the Armani out of its bag and said to Jane, "What do you think of my flash new suit?" Alas, I am color-blind. Navy blue had always been indistinguishable from black to my eyes, and I had packed not the Armani but a normal navy blue suit. In its long, indeed more than 150-year history, the Willard had had its quotient of similar dunces, and I went to the White House in a swiftly rented suit; the Armani was reserved for more mundane American and Sydney events, such as the formal evenings of the Manly-Warringah Rugby League Club.

Even so, this was an astonishing night for us. The president, being gunned-for over Arkansas real estate deals, possessed that astonishing, languid composure and the same sharpness of gaze he had had at the premiere. But it seemed both he and his wife had more time. The first lady again discussed with me my novel *Woman of the Inner Sea*. The president had, above all, a campaigner's capacity to fix you with his eye and engage you—even among old friends of his such as Paul Newman and Joanne Woodward—as if you were somehow the focus of the room. He possessed a capacity, that is, to convince you of the special relationship he had with you. I had seen this in other men before. Bob Hawke, Australian prime minister, had the same talent.

As the evening progressed I had enough time to remember that another Australian, at least an Australian by convict sentence, General Thomas Francis Meagher, had stood as honor guard here over the body of Lincoln. Yet contemporary scandals intruded on reminiscence. During the dinner, George Stephanopoulos was frequently in the dining room and at the president's ear. This was the sole sign that President Clinton and his elegant wife had enemies upon this earth.

———————

Films, as well as being good for fancy invitations, can also produce a storm front of accusations. The story that Emilie Schindler had been shortchanged in the whole process, had been taken for granted and neglected, was still around. It happened that one of the speeches I made was at a fund-raiser in Miami-Dade County, at which Emilie also made an appearance. Before the event, we were all taken to lunch by the organizers. I found myself sitting next to Erika Rosenberg, and asked her if she really believed that Emilie had not been consulted on the book and film, and had not been paid anything. With obvious sincerity, she answered, "Not a penny."

I asked her if she was sure about that; did she know a lawyer called Juan Caro? She knew Mr. Caro but still insisted, "Not a penny."

"And not a penny from the film?"

Mrs. Schindler, observing our conversation, moved forward angrily in her chair and told Rosenberg to drop the subject. The next morning, on a plane back to California, I used the phone recessed into the seat to call Spielberg's office and informed them that Rosenberg and, passively, Emilie were still pursuing the "not a penny" line. I told Steven's assistant, Chris Kelly, that I knew Rosenberg was wrong, not least because I had recently sent Emilie a check myself. Chris told me that a sum had been paid Mrs. Schindler recently, and when I asked, admitting that it was none of my business, whether it was a settlement in the thousands or tens of thousands, Chris indicated the latter. Next, still in the air, I called Emilie's old friend and Schindler's lover Ingrid, and her husband, on Long Island. They were amused by Rosenberg. "Emilie is fine," they told me.

I asked, "Should I send another check?"

"No. Rosenberg doesn't know everything. Some things are looked after here."

It seemed that Mrs. Schindler had a New York bank account which, if not sumptuous, was adequate. If so, it was simple justice to a splendid woman who strenuously maintained, in the face of the world, her rage against her miscreant husband.

Spielberg was content to ignore Rosenberg, however widely she was published. After all, he would soon be fighting off a murderous stalker of his own. But I always felt affronted by the ease with which the claim was made that Emilie had been unjustly treated. It was claimed, too, perhaps unreliably, that when Emilie died in Germany in 2001, a year of especial resonance in this account, she died impoverished.

Twenty

Invited by Spielberg, Poldek and Misia, Judy and I attended the Academy Awards together. Poldek received a splendid tribute from Spielberg, and yet there was still an avuncular disapproval in Poldek of the time Steven had taken to "wise up" and make the film. As Spielberg entered the foyer for the Governor's Ball after the awards, Poldek grabbed one of the two Oscars he'd won for direction and Best Film, an artifact of quite surprisingly heavy mass, and made as if to cuff him on the head. "What did I tell you?" demanded Poldek. "What did I tell you? An Oscar for Oskar."

I was most comfortable, of course, with the premieres in Australia—particularly the first, the Sydney premiere, to which Ben Kingsley came. A press conference was held in the Sydney Jewish Museum, a regional museum of the highest quality. I was fascinated that it commemorated the first Passover seder in Australia, in 1788, when a Jewish Cockney girl convict named Esther Abrahams was given a special ration of wine and bread to enable the Jewish convicts to observe the holiday.

The third member at the press conference was my old friend Leo Rosner, the accordionist who, with his brother Henry, had once been forced to entertain Amon Goeth day after day. That evening there was a cocktail party at the Sydney Hilton to which Leo brought his accordion. He had never heard John Williams's splendid film score before, but instantly picked up the dominant theme and played it with the orchestra there. Here was a Jew in a remote place—I don't think Hitler thought much of Sydney or Australia in his career—and the Jew was playing an accordion in the Sydney night, affirming his survival.

My father was by now elderly, and found it hard to walk from the Hilton to the cinema in Pitt Street. But to the very end of his life he remained too proud to use a wheelchair and so, painfully, we made our way across Pitt Street to the theater, aware of his pain as he asked, "How bloody far is it now?" Thus my father approached Steven Spielberg's most remarkable rendition of the Nazi regime, against which the old man had certainly "done his bit." I sat next to him in the cinema and was aware that though his eyesight was impaired and his bladder touchy, he was engrossed for three and a quarter hours.

At the Melbourne premiere, while speaking before the film, Ben Kingsley, that wonderful traveling companion, took on the Melbourne Club, the focus of the Melbourne establishment, which still had not admitted a single Jew as a member. And in that city on the next somewhat hungover day, we said good-bye to each other.

The last time I saw Poldek was in the spring of 2000. It was in his living room where Misia had always staged our high afternoon teas, with pastries and cakes and *herbata*. Poldek was suddenly having trouble walking, and that fact shocked me. He had always been such an emphatic walker, and not to have the power of locomotion stripped him of some of his purpose. "The computer is fine," he told me, tapping his head. "But the machine—it needs replacing."

I had not expected Poldek to decline so young—he was eighty-seven, but that was young for him. I wondered whether having been a prisoner had any impact upon his health. Certainly he still received a payment from the German government as compensation for the back damage the Oberscharführer who regularly beat him up in Płaszów had imposed on him. A therapist says of Holocaust survivors that as they get older and their long-term memory increases, their helplessness in old age begins to reflect their former helplessness in the camps. Poldek still seemed a very positive-minded human being, but whether the stress, the fear, the hunger of the past, had affected that boiler of a heart of his is a question that, when he was alive and vivid, many of his friends forgot to ask.

To what extent was he, too, haunted? Did he, in the delirium of his passing, think even for a moment that he was subject to Amon Goeth, and grist for the cruel laws which had once sought to take away his oxygen? Common sense would have to say that not even Poldek could have escaped some permanent damage, some abiding erosion. So that perhaps his greatest success, even greater than turning Schindler into a modern legend, was to be able to live a normal life in normal streets, such as South Elm Drive in "California, Beverly Hills."

That year in which Poldek was declining, my ninety-two-year-old father's health was deteriorating too, in a slow collapse of the various functions of the body. But again it was impossible to believe that this amusingly profane, bush-eloquent patriarch could stop breathing.

My father, as was natural to him, gave death a hard run. For weeks he fought. A young priest came to give him communion, and they said the Our Father together. A sad thing to see a larrikin, a boy from the bush, humbly uttering those ancient sentiments to the Deity! No sooner was "Amen" out of his mouth than he added, "Well, Father, I think I'm bloody rooted." This was his Australian *Nunc Dimittis*, his version of "Now let Thy servant depart in peace . . ."

He died on a bitter August day. At his funeral, a man from the Returned Services League described him as "the good sergeant," and the consonance between that and the old usage of "good sergeant" as an image of death set off howls of grief in his smart-alec son's mind, and the tears came and were not readily staunched.

From halfway through the Sydney Olympics in September until Christmas I was useless and finished, physically and mentally. Some years before, a commentator in a literary and political magazine had prematurely written a piece with a title like "Thomas Keneally, My Role in His Destruction." But it had taken factors more universal and more forceful than mean faction-fighting to make me believe I was, indeed, finished.

As I had my crisis, I did not know Poldek was having his. He was at one with my father in that he didn't believe in making a fuss when he got sick. He had gone full of confidence to Cedars-Sinai hospital in Beverly Hills, but there his end was fast. In March 2001, an email appeared on my computer from Poldek's daughter, Marie, saying that he had died in the hospital, apparently quite suddenly. So both the old heroes were improbably dead! My own health and the practice of prompt Jewish burial kept me from Poldek's funeral. I sent a message of profound regret and in it told the story of his indomitability, of traveling to Poland with him under the protection of his Orbis badge. It was read in the chapel of the Hillside Memorial Park where Poldek was buried. As a sign of resignation, Misia put a stone on her husband's grave. At the time I write this she is still living, sixty years after—as a medical student in Vienna—she saw Hitler triumphantly enter the city. One of her comrades from Auschwitz and Brinnlitz, Sydney's Leosia Korn (Losia the Optimist in the book), has recently died.

These days, writing again, feeling more robust, I do not easily forgive myself for failing to have seen Poldek into the grave, to the lip of which, he had told me, we would be brothers. He died a man without enemies, and with the knowledge that his easily dismissed predictions had come true almost by his own force of personality. The Righteous Persons Foundation was quick, with Steven Spielberg's assistance, in endowing a series of lectures at Chapman University in Poldek's name. Many of his documents and photographs are in the

National Holocaust Museum in Washington. The *Los Angeles Times* honored him in an obituary as the initiator of the entire process with which this tale has concerned itself.

What did I tell you? he would have asked. What *did* I tell you?

The text of this book is set in Filosofia, created in 1984 by Zuzana Licko, who co-founded *Emigre* magazine with her husband, Rudy RanderLans. Filosofia is a digital typeface created with the first generation of the Macintosh computer. Its popularity in *Emigre* led to the establishment of Emigre Fonts.